CRYSTALS FOR BEGINNERS

Meditation Techniques, Reiki and Healing Stones! The Power of Crystal Healing! How to Enhance Your Chakras-Spiritual Balance and Human Energy Field

BY

Cassian Byrd

TABLE OF CONTENTS

COPYRIGHTS 6

CHAPTER 1: INTRODUCTION 10
- ➤ **RENAISSANCE** 13
- ➤ **WHAT ARE THE HEALING CRYSTALS?** 17

CHAPTER 2: THE HEALING POWER OF CRYSTALS AND HEALING STONES 21
- ➤ **HOW DOES IT WORK?** 23
- ➤ **HOW TO CHOOSE CRYSTAL?** 27

CHAPTER 3: THE POWER OF CRYSTAL HEALING TO ENHANCE YOUR CHAKRAS- SPIRITUAL BALANCE- HUMAN ENERGY FIELD 30
- ➤ **A POWERFUL CHAKRA BALANCE COMBINATION CAN INCLUDE THE FOLLOWING CRYSTALS:** ... 32

- **BENEFITS OF SPIRITUAL CRYSTALS AND HOW TO USE THEM:** 36
- **SPIRITUAL CRYSTALS DEEPEN YOUR MEDITATION PRACTICE:** 40
- **WHY ARE EARTHING AND PROTECTION IMPORTANT?** 44

CHAPTER 4: MEDITATION TECHNIQUES AND REIKI HEALING 51

- **REASONS TO APPLY CRYSTALS IN REIKI** 54

CHAPTER 5: CRYSTAL & CHAKRA CORRESPONDENCES 62
.... 62

- **CRYSTAL HEALING**
- **THE PRIMARY FEMININE ENERGY CRYSTALS AND GEMS ARE:** 81
- **BASIC CRYSTAL HEALING BAGS THE BEST ENERGY CRYSTALS**

- **AND GEMSTONES FOR KIDS ARE:** 81
- **SOME OF THE CENTRAL STONES AND CRYSTALS OF ANIMAL ENERGY ARE:** 82
- **BENEFITS OF CRYSTAL HEALING** 87
- **HERE ARE THE MORE IDEAS TO PRACTICE THESE GEMSTONES FOR HEALING? HERE ARE THE STEP-BY-STEP PROCEDURES:** 100
- **HOW TO USE CRYSTAL HEALING?** 102
- **PROGRAMMING METHODS** 107
- **TIPS AND TECHNIQUES FOR HARDENING ABANDONED CRYSTALS** 109

CONCLUSION 272

COPYRIGHTS 275

COPYRIGHTS

© Copyright 2020 By Cassian Byrd
All rights reserved

This book
"CRYSTALS FOR BEGINNERS: Meditation Techniques, Reiki and Healing Stones! The Power of Crystal Healing! How to Enhance Your Chakras-Spiritual Balance and Human Energy Field
Written by Cassian Byrd

This document aims to provide precise and reliable details on this subject and the problem under discussion.

The product is marketed on the assumption that no officially approved bookkeeping or publishing house provides other available funds.

Where a legal or qualified guide is required, a person must have the right to participate in the field.

A statement of principle, which is a subcommittee of the American Bar Association, a committee of publishers and Associations and approved. A copy, reproduction, or distribution of parts of this text, in electronic or written form, is not permitted.

The recording of this Document is strictly prohibited, and any retention of this text is only with the written permission of the publisher and all Liberties authorized.

The information provided here is correct and reliable, as any lack of attention or other means resulting from the misuse or use of the procedures, procedures, or instructions contained therein is the total, and absolute obligation of the user addressed.

The author is not obliged, directly or indirectly, to assume civil or civil liability for any restoration, damage, or loss resulting from the data collected here. The respective authors retain all copyrights not kept by the publisher.

The information contained herein is solely and universally available for information purposes. The data is presented without a warranty or promise of any kind.

The trademarks used are without approval, and the patent is issued without the trademark owner's permission or protection.

The logos and labels in this book are the property of the owners themselves and are not associated with this text.

CHAPTER 1: INTRODUCTION

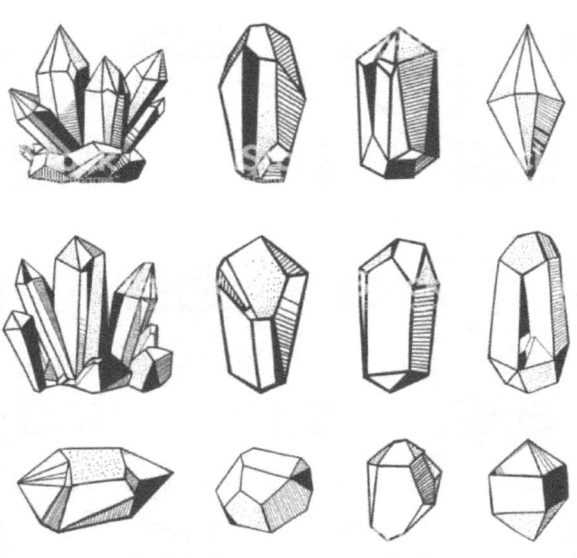

As long as our history goes, we humans are very much familiar with stones and crystals. Amulets and the use of charms date back to the origins of humanity, but we do not know that at the early stages, how these objects were displayed or used. Many of the early works were of organic origin. The pearls carved from mammoth ivory has excavated from a 60,000year-old tomb in Sangyr-Bulak (Paleolithic Old Town), Russia.

The first historical evidence of the use of crystals comes from the ancient antiquity of the Sumerians; they included crystals in the magic formula. The biblical Egyptians practiced lapis lazuli, carnelian, turquoise, emeralds, and clear quartz for their gems. They also carved a tomb talisman from the same gemstones. Ancient Egyptians used stone primarily for protection and health. Chrysolite (later translated into Topaz and Peridot) has applied to fight the nightly horrors and eliminate demons. Egyptians also used crystals in cosmetics. Galena (lead ore) was ground into an explosive and used as an eye shadow called cabbage. Malachite used for this purpose as well. Green stones had commonly used to mark the heart of the deceased and had included in the burial.

Green stones later used in a similar way in ancient Mexico.

Ancient Greeks attribute many properties to crystals, and many of the names used today derive from Greek. The word "crystal" originates from the Greek term ice. Clear quartz is supposed to be water that freezes very rapidly and remains stable at all temperatures. The word amethyst means "not drunk" and was worn as a talisman to prevent sickness and hangovers. Hematite comes from the word blood because it rotates when it oxidizes. Hematite is iron ore, and the ancient Greeks linked the god of war, Aries, to iron. Before the battle, the Greek soldiers rubbed hematite against their bodies and immortalized themselves. Greek sailors also wore various amulets to protect them at sea.

Jade has highly regarded in ancient China, and some Chinese characters represent jade pearls. The chime instrument has made from jade, and the emperor of China was sometimes buried in the jade tank about 1000 years ago. In Mexico, there is a burial with a jade mask of the same period. Jade has recognized as a kidney healing stone in both China and South America. More recently, about 250 years ago, New Zealand's Maori tribe wore a Jade pendant that represented the spirit of their ancestors and was inherited by men's lineage for many generations. The tradition that green stones are lucky continues to this day in parts of New Zealand.

RENAISSANCE

From the 11th century to the Renaissance, numerous medical articles have been published in Europe, highlighting the benefits of precious and semiprecious stones in the treatment of certain diseases. Stones are used in combination with herbal remedies for treatments. Authors who wrote on this subject include Hildegard von Bingen,

Arnoldas Saxo, and John Mandeville. There are also signs of stones with exceptional strength and protective properties. In 1232, Henry III's Supreme Judge, Hubert Doberberg, stole jewels from the King's Treasury, gave them secrets, and passed them to the enemies of Kings of Wales, Llewellyn, and Henry. We also believe that Adam's original sin destroyed the gem and perhaps lost the virtue when the devil lived or has treated by a sinner. Therefore, it must be sanctified and consecrated before it can be worn. This belief is reflected today in the cleansing and programming of crystals before their use in crystal healing.

Crystal healing affects the vibration and energy level of the crystal as it repairs problems, areas, and trends in the vibration energy field. Crystal healing is not a new art and does not require any special training to perform this kind of task. But before you start, you need to be careful about the doorways. Crystal Healing balances a person's energy and provides balance in the body, relieving problems, or treats imbalances in front of them. Today, there are so many crystals and gems in the world. The use of diamonds and gemstones can be very confusing unless you study, learn, and practice them yourself. This book contains 555 different tips on some of the most common illnesses, problems, and difficulties we face in the body.

I have shared and used all these 555 tips with my family, friends, customers, and colleagues. Books on Practical Crystal Healing techniques and basic crystal books can be found online at bookstores and courses. They provide excellent information on the basics of crystals. This has explained in detail in this book. It also contains colorful photos, background information, hardness tests, and other related properties. However, the proper use of crystals is essential. If you don't know how to use it, try another method; otherwise, you won't get any results. This book is different because it explains how to use crystals and gems for a particular purpose related to it. As with most things in life, healing of crystals has not guaranteed at all. You have to work at it, practice it, and find the one that suits you. When crystals are used at those specific points, as described in this book, Crystal Healing will not harm you or your body.

The healing and energy of all types of crystals have always done for the best effect and most positive results. Understand that many crystals are used for all kinds of diseases, problems, or difficulties we are facing. I set a task myself to find the best answer to solve these problems. Therefore, there are no fluffs or fillers here! Everyone has different vibration battles and challenges. So, use them at your will and understand that the healing issues are different from each other and also differs from person to person. The use of crystals is a part of the healing process. Enjoy the healing, and let the crystals work for you!

For thousands of years, people of all classes have been healing with crystals, from ancient Sumerians to modern yogis. Each crystal has its vibration and healing properties. Some crystals heal the body, while others nourish the mind and promote better relationships and harmony in life. Conclusion: Almost all classes of society believe in healing crystals! Are you ready for your healing journey?

This Crystal Healing Guide examines the best healing crystals and explains which type of crystals can be helpful to heal the illness and how you can use them to live a healthier and happier life.

WHAT ARE THE HEALING CRYSTALS?

Healing crystals are natural stones in which the goals, intentions, and dreams of life have revealed. These mysterious crystals use the higher power of the Earth's elements like the sun, the moon, the sea, and the universe to bring healing energy inside. Healing Crystals are not magic stones that change your life overnight. Instead, they are gems that heals your body and soul. As discovered by scientist Marcel Vogel, it is a remnant of the Earth with molecular vibrations that preserve information. When the owner expresses specific intents or hopes, crystals reinforce and emphasize these intents.

While Vogel clarified the powerful energy of healing crystals in the 20th century, civilizations have been using them for thousands of years as an amulet of happiness and protection. The ancient Egyptians demanded protection and health and dressed in lapis lazuli and clear quartz to ward off evil spirits. With a fast forward of 5,000 years to date, people are still using crystals to provide healing in every aspect of their lives. Let's dig deeper into the best healing crystals and their meaning.

CHAPTER 2: THE HEALING POWER OF CRYSTALS AND HEALING STONES

Crystal healing is an alternative medical technique that uses crystals and other stones to cure and protect against illness. The proponents of this technique believe that crystals act as channels for healing-when the fever that causes harmful disease subsides when positive healing energy flows into the body.

Although crystal healing has become more and more popular in recent years, this alternative treatment is not popular with most doctors and scientists, many of the scientists call crystal healing, a pseudoscience. There are no accurate pieces of evidence that gem healing can be used to treat a disease. This is because it has shown that this condition is not the result of the so-called energy flow in the body. Moreover, scientific studies have not shown that crystals and gems can be distinguished by chemical composition or color for the treatment of certain diseases. Nevertheless, Healing Crystals are known in health spas and New Age Health Clinics and are included in related massage techniques and reiki practices. Using crystals in such an environment can contribute to relaxation, but this effect is not supported by scientific evidence either.

HOW DOES IT WORK?

Crystal healing advocates believe that crystals and gems have healing properties. Many places that promote crystal healing have an ancient history of this practice, dating back to at least 6,000 years in the Sumerian era of Mesopotamia. Ancient Egyptians sought to prevent disease and negative energy, including the first place to garnish with crystals such as lapis lazuli, carnelian, and turquoise. However, the modern philosophy of crystal healing based on the traditional notions of Asian culture, in particular the concept of Chinese life energy (qi) and the idea of Hindu or Buddhist chakras. This vital energy vortex connects the physical and supernatural elements of the body.

In crystal healing, stones have different properties, but healers also have other ideas about different properties each stone has. For example, some people think of beneficial amethyst for the intestines. Green Aventurine helps the heart. Yellow Topaz guarantees mental clarity. Red to purple colors combined with the seven chakra points on the body. During a healing session, a crystal healer can place a variety of stones and crystals aligned to these chakra points on the head, forehead, neck, chest, and stomach, mostly in the intestines, genital area. The stones used and their placement can be selected depending on the symptoms reported by the patient. All this is influenced by the healer's knowledge and beliefs about the sick chakra philosophy and energy imbalance. Western medicine practitioners have primarily rejected this philosophy.

Crystal healing also includes the use of crystals or stones that can be worn on the body or placed under a pillow to drive off illness, drop off negative energy, and to absorb positive energy.

THE ACTUAL MECHANISM:

Although there are no scientific studies on the effectiveness of crystal healing, one research suggests that crystal healing may have a placebo effect in patients undergoing this type of treatment. The placebo effect is treatment-related, not directly related to the procedure that affects the patient's disease, says Christopher French, director of abnormal psychology at the University of London.

"There is no indication that quartz restorative functioning beyond the placebo effect," French told Live Science. "This is a good criterion for determining any form of treatment, but whether crystal healing or any other type of "complementary and alternative medicine" is of no value depends on the placebo effect. It depends on your attitude. As the French emphasized, there are many treatments known to have no therapeutic effect other than placebo. Although these treatments can temporarily make you feel better, there is no evidence that they can treat illnesses or health problems. According to French, if you have a severe medical problem, you should be treated by a qualified doctor, not an alternative therapist.

IS CRYSTAL HEALING SAFE?

Anyone who is interested in this technique can become a healer by passing the accredited courses offered online by the University of Natural Medicine and clinics. Currently, there aren't state or federal laws that explicitly regulate or standardize the behavior of Crystal Healers or the Crystal Healer licenses. In some states, these types of alternative treatments fall into the category of massage or body therapy. In these states, crystal healers may require a license to practice.

Non-profit organizations also conduct voluntary certification exams for massage therapists and alternative therapists. NCTMB supports schools and companies that qualify as alternative therapists only if they meet specific criteria set by the organization.

HOW TO CHOOSE CRYSTAL?

If you want to choose a crystal for personal use, you should use at least primary colors. This includes orange, red, green, yellow, blue, purple, pink, white, transparent, and black. Crystal color is associated with the center of the chakra and may be related to several diseases. It is advised to put various crystals and gems in your fingers when working. My personal favorites are Peridot, Hematite, Red Jasper, Rose Quartz, Rhodonite, Carnelian, Topaz, Amber, Tiger

Eyes, Malachite, Bloodstone, Moss Agate, Turquoise, Aquamarine, Lapis Lazuli, Amethyst, Fluorite, Clear quartz, moonstone, onyx, black tourmaline, and smoky quartz.

There are many crystals and gems. So, don't be overwhelmed or confused when choosing the one that suits you. The best guide for choosing a practical crystal healing crystal is to follow intuition. You may have heard that your intuition never misleads you. Even if you never worked with the "intuition" instinct, it can be challenging when using it. When choosing a new crystal, make sure it feels good, and you are happy. I don't want to attract negative and energetic emotions, so put some lively music in the car and think about the fun of going to a glass shop. Once you get there, go and look around and make sure that you are going for the first eye-catcher. Pick up the crystal and see if it suits you. If so, look for more to add to your Crystal Healing Kit. If not, leave it there and do not burden yourself with it. There are no correct or incorrect answers, but what resonates with you! Remember to choose as many of your crystals as you like!

CHAPTER 3: THE POWER OF CRYSTAL HEALING TO ENHANCE YOUR CHAKRAS- SPIRITUAL BALANCE- HUMAN ENERGY FIELD

Each chakra on the body has assigned to a specific area and color. Many healing stones and crystals can use to purify, revive, and balance chakra energy. This method is based on the fact that the chakra stone has an energy field. The vibrations are guided and amplified by all crystals and resonate with specific energy centers in your body.

A POWERFUL CHAKRA BALANCE COMBINATION CAN INCLUDE THE FOLLOWING CRYSTALS:

Amethyst, the healing stone, provides clearing, cleansing, and protective energy to the crown chakra.

Jasper is an ideal tool to overcome deferral or delay by showing the exact reason to avoid a particular task and providing the motivation to solve the problem. And it's great for balancing the chakras of the solar plexus.

Lapis lazuli, a powerful crystal that activates your hearts and improves intellectual abilities. Ideal for improving memory. Lapis lazuli balances the third eye chakra.

A rock crystal is a crystal that helps to improve self-esteem. This beautiful crystal can also absorb and take in the energy of other crystals.

Agate that stabilizes the aura also removes negative energy and transforms it. It can be used in 1st to 4th chakras.

The Tiger's Eye, a powerful stone that promotes harmony and balance, and helps soothe anxiety and calmness. Promotes the intuition of the solar plexus chakra and enhances the mental abilities of the third eye chakra.

Green Aventurine is a comforter, heart healer, purifier which activates the heart chakra, providing general well-being and emotional calmness. Therefore, it is said that do not underestimate the healing powers of natural crystals.

People think they are likely to believe in the healing properties of crystals or try to pick a stick from the floor to cast magic.

Healing power and its use may seem magical, but crystals have a scientific background. Although crystals are still considered an alternative to healing, it's quite logical to say that why crystals do what they do. Crystals oscillate at their frequencies, just as cells and chakras in their bodies oscillate at their rates.

It means that when they come in contact with crystals, these different frequencies meet and improve the physical, emotional, and mental health.

Crystals have a fantastic ability to transform, absorb, enhance, and transmit. Energy is everywhere, and crystals have perfect conduction ability. It is known that the vibration of a crystal changes depending on the point surrounding the crystal, and each stone has different effects. It has developed initially to balance the chakras and transform the energy and properties of the body; crystal therapy provides a clear and definite energy field. When it comes to crystals, it is believed that when it heals and restores the energy that flows naturally through your body, it actually improves your body.

Black onyx gemstones are powerful protective stones that absorb and transform negative energy. It improves nervous and mechanical durability, particularly when support has needed during stress, confusion, and sadness. Black onyx is a dominant mass that helps make smart decisions and develop healthy habits by focusing on balance. This gem is also known to help disconnect oneself from dissatisfied or problematic people and situations. Onyx preserves, restore, and stimulates the source chakra, making it more grounded, creative, and productive in the physical world.

Recognized as one of the several significant rocks in the heart chakra, rose quartz is often used for its healing properties as it promotes unconditional love.

However, it can also be used to balance all chakras and release them from negative energy. If used with positive self-affirmation, it helps build trust and acceptance. It is also the most frequently used crystal because of its healing properties. This stone's gentle energy helps to create an environment in which you feel nourished, supported, and able to perform your daily tasks more efficiently. It is a crystal known for forgiveness and compassion. Nature provides powerful tools that support us in our spiritual efforts, and these tools are pure crystals. These high-vibration stones provide intangible benefits and help to develop our mental talents and abilities. Let's take a look at these fascinating advantages and how to use pure crystals to improve your spiritual condition.

BENEFITS OF SPIRITUAL CRYSTALS AND HOW TO USE THEM:

Spiritual crystals are those spiritual gems that help to connect the mind, body, and spirit. To improve one side of your life, you need to improve the other. It is impossible because our hearts are the interwoven tapestries. There is nothing that can represent itself independently because the aspects of the mind, body, and soul have incorporated. When we have a headache, it is a physical symptom that often results from mental elements such as stress, and it can have a mental aspect too. When we are happy, we feel energized and connected to the world. It feels like my physical strength is unsatisfactory when I eat a lot, but I am trying to connect mental and physical health. We have several examples to show the connection between mind, body, and soul works. It is essential to know that the problem will persist until the root causes of the problem cannot be found. Physical symptoms are rarely physical. Mental crystals help heal physical, mental, and emotional wounds. Heart chakra stones such as Rose Quartz, Emerald, and Rhodonite are suitable for mental health and support and a loving and gentle nature. Lepidolite is an ideal stone for mental health as it eliminates stress, anxiety, and cloudy thoughts. Amazonite helps reduce anger, and citrine brings luck. Concerning physical dissatisfaction, a little research can reveal which stone is useful for which part of the body. For example, red jasper helps the cardiovascular system. Rhodonite eliminates cold, and flu symptoms and yellow crystals help improve digestive health.

There are many stones known for their spiritual benefits. Amethyst and azurite, for example, help to adjust our intuition. Rutile Quartz helps spiritual awakening and light help to connect with the spiritual world. But these stones are not specified only to affect the physical, mental or spiritual aspects of the body. For example, if a stone is known to contribute to mental health, it also involves certain physical and mental aspects of health as well. They all are interconnected.

Because spirituality, physical and mental health are inextricably linked, it is always best to choose a comprehensive approach for crystal healing. You can use the individual crystals together to support yourself and heal the root cause of the problem. Spiritual crystals involve the ignition of violet frame vibration.

Amethyst symbolizes the vibration of a purple flame, also called the purple beam. It turns the body's negative energy into light and love. This healing wave is governed by the Ascended Master Saint Germain, who lived in the 16th century and dedicated his life to healing others from negative energies. The vibration of the purple flame removes negative energy from the body and protects us from negative beings and psychological attacks. It can access by holding amethyst stones in the presence of Amethyst Geode or by wearing amethyst jewelry and asking Saint Germain for help. Most purple stones such as tanzanite, purple Sugilite, and purple perlite have purple frame vibration, but amethyst is the strongest among these. Amethyst has high-frequency vibrations that help us discover and access our spirituality easier and faster. By placing these healing stones on the aura, shifts the energy to higher frequencies.

SPIRITUAL CRYSTALS DEEPEN YOUR MEDITATION PRACTICE:

Meditation is one of the most important things you can do to improve your spirituality. It brings us closer to the higher self and facilitates the transition to a deeper state of consciousness. Meditation with crystals further enhances these results. Meditation crystals help us to calm, purify negative energies, remove chakras, improve our intuition, and also guide us spiritually. Spiritual gems connect us to a higher spirit. Spiritual Crystals strengthen our connection with our higher self, our leaders, our angels, and God. We all have a variety of mental communication methods that are unique to us. Fluoroscopy is when you can see a guide or have a vision. Clairaudience is when you hear a ghost speak. Perspective is when you feel something in your body, and it helps you to recognize it. Fluoroscopy is just about what you know, not how you know it. Spiritual crystals help to improve these natural methods. Purple perlite and prehnite are the perfect crystals to connect and communicate with your guides and angels. They help us to hear, see, feel, and know what they are saying to us. Other crystals that are particularly useful in making a connection with High Spirits are Rainbow Fluorite, Clear Quartz, Rainbow Moonstone, Angelite, Azurite, and Lepidolite.

PURE CRYSTALS AWAKEN KUNDALINI

Awakening of Kundalini occurs when the energy of Kundalini moves the spine from the base chakra to the crown chakra. The Kundalini snake, located at the base of the spine, awakens and climbs at the crown chakra, signifies a movement of enlightenment. Various pure crystals support Kundalini's awakening process, such as Shiveringham, Tiger Eye, Moldavite, and Red Jasper. Serpentine eliminates most of the illnesses and problems that can occur when Kundalini wakes up.

HOW ARE SPIRITUAL CRYSTALS RELATED TO THE CHAKRAS?

THIRD EYE CRYSTAL

The third eye is the physical center of energy that manages our intuition and perspective. When it is open and turns optimally, we feel a connection with the inner knowledge. It can be expressed by intuition, spiritual vision, listening to messages, or merely knowing things. You should Recognize your control system, make better decisions, stay in the right place at the right time, and follow your life. However, you may need help to open and balance the third eye chakra. This is where the third eye crystal comes into play. The third eye crystal is a spiritual crystal that opens the third eye chakra. When we wear, hold, and bring them into the energy sector, they help to evoke the interests of all third parties. The spiritual crystals associated with the third-eye chakra tend to be purple, including amethyst, purple fluorspar, and sugilite. Other non-purple crystals of the third eye include obsidian, moldavite, lapis lazuli, and azurite.

CROWN CHAKRA CRYSTAL

The Crown Chakra is a physical energy center that manages your connection to higher consciousness. This is how you connect with your guides, angels, and higher self. Crown chakra stones help us live with our values. They bring us strong empathy and selflessness and promote intelligence, wisdom, and psychological knowledge. These crystals open the crown chakra, further improving communication between the psyche and higher consciousness. By strengthening our spiritual connection, we experience a more "unity." These coincidences can provide spiritual guidance. You know something is telling you to take another way home, and you will miss the accident. The same quote appears everywhere. Or meet old industry friends you want to go to. Crown chakra crystals include amethyst, clear quartz, rutile quartz, selenite, Herkimer diamonds, and ametrine.

WHY ARE EARTHING AND PROTECTION IMPORTANT?

When we focus on spirituality, it becomes easy to lose ground, and this imbalance can cause physical and mental health problems. You have to deal with psychological attacks too. It is where ground stones and protection stones come into play. Some foundations are bronze, hematite, dragon stone, smoky quartz, garnet, and petrified wood.

All crystals and gems should be washed before use. It is not possible to see where they from, who collects them, what is suitable for their energy field, or what kind of energy is already associated with them. Therefore, the first thing to do when you bring a crystal home is to clean them! There are several ways to clean a new glass. Dirt can be washed, mother earth energy, sage tea washes, solar energy, sound vibrations, mirror energy, and even sand washes can be used as needed. For cleaning the stained stone, it is the smoke of the stained bar that can be used.

Dirt from pure sage or a combination of sages is excellent for cleaning crystals. Pass them through the dirty smoke at least four times left and right. Cleaning the stone with water and sea salt is very easy. For harder crystals, you can place them in a small glass container of Crystal Healing 6 brine for at least 1 hour. For softer gems, you can spray thoroughly with a water spray to completely cover the crystals and allow them to drain well. Using the energy of Mother Earth is easy and fun. But it is a dirty way to clean your stone. Pick up the crystal, wrap it in pure chiffon, and wrap it again in a silk cloth. Find a special place in your garden where you can bury the new stone.

Dig a 6-8-inch hole in the ground and place the stone in it. Cover it, mark it, and so you should be able to dig! After 24 hours, clear the stone and gently rinse to lose dirt. Sage Tea Cleaning is a fun and safe way to incorporate several different aspects into your crystal's powerful cleaning session. Prepare sage, prepare fresh sage, and make tea from fresh sage. Let it cool and put the stone in a glass container. Pour tea with sage into a glass container and soak overnight. It combines dirt strength and water energy to clean dirt. Be sure to wash the stone in the morning! Solar power and water can also be used to clean the stone. To do this, maintain the stone beneath the running water stream for 1 minute and then place the stone in the sun to dry. Do not place it in direct sunshine for a long time, as some crystals may fade in direct sunlight. It takes only a few minutes to dry, so keep an eye on it.

It is simple to clean diamonds and gems using the energy of the mirror. Simply place the stone on top of the mirror and put it on a table or cupboard so that the mirror reflects the heat already carried by the stone. Allow this to remain in the mirror for at least 24 hours. You can also use the sand method for almost any type of crystal or gemstone. Cover the gems in moist sand and leave for at least 2 hours. This should only be used as an end resource, as sand can remove some of the glazes from the crystals. Whether you use the gem in a healing session or the crystal rack, you should clean the gem regularly. Each problem is different and needs to be considered differently depending on what the healing or grid accomplished in the task. As a basic rule of thumb, always clean the crystals after each healing session. When using the grid location, cleaning can be done from once a week to once a month. The stones used should be cleaned and reprogrammed every 24 hours if necessary. Follow the guidelines in this book for the best results. If you use Crystal Healing consistently, keep in mind that the Crystal should also heal itself. It is always a good idea to send crystals to Mother Earth for at least a month during the calendar years in which they have frequently used. It means you should bury them in Mother Earth and restore their vibrational healing. Mark, where you bury them and mark date on your calendar to remind you when to rediscover them!

CHAPTER 4: MEDITATION TECHNIQUES AND REIKI HEALING

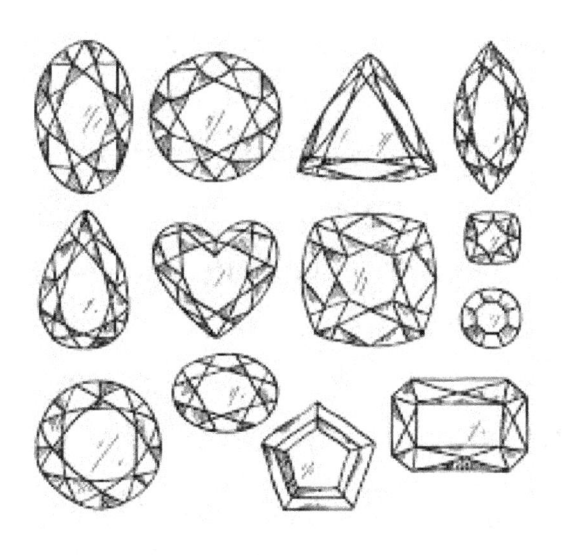

Meditation with crystals is a two-step process. First, you need to find a crystal with universal life energy that corresponds to your intention. Then you need to hold the crystal or put it in front of you so that you can focus on it during meditation. Choosing the right crystal requires some research. Each crystal has an energy grid of it, a color beam of influence, and the Earth's forces that result from its chemical composition. Choose the one with the energy that suits your needs. Seeker Crystals and Unifier Crystals are particularly suitable. The mirror is also excellent.

It is also possible to use crystals with the required Feng Shui elemental energy. Such crystals can be found in the Feng Shui section. There are crystals that are strong against the essential power of water, soil, fire, metal, and wood. You can also use crystals that target spiritual guidance, angels, or goddesses. When meditating for self-healing, you need a crystal attached to the corresponding chakra. Suggested meditation crystals and their use can be found in the description of the gems in this book.

Once you have the crystal with proper energy to perform meditation, place it in front of you, or hold it. You don't have to sit in the lotus position to meditate. You should sit comfortably. You can sit on a pillow, a chair, a bench, or anywhere you feel comfortable. Relax. Take a little deep breath. Now start from your toes and concentrate on every part of your body ready to relax fully. Focus on each piece until you come up with the time. Then count very slowly from 10 to 1. Here you see a cord that connects to the center of the Earth and extends through the Earth to the backbone, and mind. Don't get up. You shouldn't. You are now grounded and in meditation.

Crystal Reiki uses crystals with Reiki to heal your mind, body, and soul. It makes sense because crystals have been used for a long time to cure illnesses and other problems related to physical, mental, and spiritual issues. Every Reiki practitioner does a slightly different exercise, but some will place crystals around you or on top of you to start your healing session. You can also listen to soft music during the healing session. Before we get to know what, our problems and expectations are and how our Crystal Reiki's session work, you might talk practitioner.

REASONS TO APPLY CRYSTALS IN REIKI

Some Reiki practitioners say that using crystals is like another hand. As a result, some Reiki therapists will either incorporate Crystal into their practice or may offer Crystal Reiki as a separate service from Reiki. Choose a crystal according to your needs. For example, yellow stones help to balance the solar plexus chakras, and blue opal or chrysocolla help to balance the neck chakras. The therapist supports all chakras so you can use clear crystals.

HOW DOES CRYSTAL REIKI WORK?

In a typical 45-60-minute Crystal Reiki session, a therapist will move around you, placing his hands on you, shedding energy, and balancing your chakras. What you experience during a session is very personal, as it depends on why you are getting treatment and what the therapist has suggested for your treatment.

The therapist can place crystals or stones on or around the table. Larger crystals may place under the table for your comfort. After the session, ask the therapist what gem did he use. A therapist can also recommend you gems, so you can keep them at home to balance your chakras and promote self-healing.

Crystal programming or loading is a way of manipulating the crystal and transmitting the vibration level and what happens when you hold a stone at a particular vibration level and what you want to do at the vibration level while holding the stone. There are several different ways to program or load them, but simplicity is the best! The passive method is one of the easiest ways to program a crystal or gemstone. This can be done simply by using the same stone for the same purpose. For example, suppose you want to use a specific amethyst during a meditation session. This crystal is being used over and over again for the same purpose. In doing so, this will program the stone over time for your particular problem, and it will help you in your spiritual quest. Current methods require a little more focus and concentration, but it may be fun, using your thoughts, intentions, strength, and attention while projecting what you want to achieve with this particular crystal or gemstone. For this to work, your intent must be in harmony with the stone. For example, current methods cannot be used to program amethyst to use it in grounding operations. It is because these two vibration levels do not correspond, and the programming is not "fixed" to the stone. But I recommend using the "Active Method" in

Amethyst for problems like headache, intuition, insomnia, and many other reasons. For these reasons, vibration levels do not match because grounding is not an attribute for manipulating amethyst. You can also load Reiki with crystals and gems. This improves the crystal's natural powers and creates a secure connection between you and the crystal. To do this, you must at least tune to Reiki level I. Alternatively; you can have someone in sync with Reiki to charge the stone. It's a simple and easy task. Take a crystal or gem between your palms and start the flow of Reiki. Then the crystals will heal and ask that you have access to this Reiki energy for yourself and to help you in your purposes. Continue to use Reiki energy until the power drawn from the crystal disappears. Some crystals come in all tones and colors you can think of. Colors such as red and orange do not determine their ability to heal and vibrate, but they have color references associated with them. There are crystals and gems of different colors, which are always new. For crystal color references with multiple Colors, you can see the primary colors, or you can combine various color attributes. Red crystals stimulate, rejuvenate, and energize your body. Some of them also provide protection and courage. Red is linked with the source chakra and aids in the ability to use practical skills and physical survival. The orange crystals are a mixture of red and yellow, combining red energy with yellow focus energy. Orange is linked with the sacral chakra and links crystal healing with creativity, expressive questions, personal strength, and self-esteem energy flow. Yellow crystals are perfect for inspiration, concentration, happiness, and satisfaction issues. This color is associated with the solar plexus chakras, helping those who are on the path of physical and mental life and struggling with their issues, and with the ability to identify significant problems. Green crystals are commonly known as healing stones, but they are not limited to green. This color is associated with the heart chakra and works on themes of emotions, relationships, prosperity, balance, love, and personal space. Blue crystals are commonly known in all forms of communication and are associated with the throat chakra. It also works effectively on cleansing, emotional relief, and expression issues. Purple crystals have a kind of mysterious quality associated with them. They deal with the area of understanding, intuition, and peace concerning the Third Eye Chakra. Inspiration, imagination, subconsciousness, and rebalancing are also great attributes of this color.

White, transparent crystals are commonly associated with the crown chakra. They share attributes with clarity, cleanliness, cleansing, and supernatural powers. Black crystals absorb light. They are associated with grounding problems, negative repulsion, self-control, and protection. The omega chakra is attributed to this color and its associated properties. Pink crystals have soft and relaxing properties. They have linked to the heart chakra as a second color, and these crystals are the basis of energy. Its traits generally help to awake calm and gentle feelings. It also solves problems associated with love and determination. Multi-colored crystals are very common in individual crystal families. Their color match is based on a combination of related colors and their particular features.

CHAPTER 5: CRYSTAL & CHAKRA CORRESPONDENCES

The correlation between chakras and crystals is easy to understand and use. It is believed that the chakras are the energy centers of our whole body, and they make a continuous flow of our life energy possible! Etherified has seven major chakras, over 300 minor chakras, and multiple ascended chakras. Each chakra has a corresponding color and unique properties. Mixing up this and features of the crystal, it's easy to see how the healing of the crystal can help initiate the path of spiritual healing. You don't have to understand every crystal and every chakra attribute to work on healing. For healing and use of the chakra, place a crystal or gem of the appropriate color on or over the chakra area during meditation or healing sessions. This activates the chakras, clears obstacles, and allows adjustment of all energy centers.

CRYSTAL HEALING

MINOR CHAKRA
It is in the arch of both legs. Agate, brown calcite, brown carnelian, and chalcedony quartz are perfect for this chakra.

OMEGA CHAKRA
It is below the root chakra between the ether energy field, and the thigh Onyx, obsidian,

hematite, and black tourmaline are perfect for this chakra.

ROOT CHAKRA
It resides at the bottom of the spine. Red Jasper, ruby, garnet, and magnetic stone are perfect for this chakra.

HOLY CHAKRA
It is on the navel or directly below the navel. Carnelian, orange jasper, citrine, and topaz are perfect for this chakra.

HAND CHAKRA
Small chakra: It is located on the palms of both hands. You can use attractive crystals with the hand chakra. If you feel difficulty in decision making, you can always use this clear crystal for this chakra. Always trust your intuition when choosing a crystal!

SOLAR PLEXUS CHAKRA

Large Chakra: It is located above the navel and below the chest. Yellow calcite, yellow jasper, amber, and tiger's eyes are perfect for this chakra.

SPLEEN CHAKRA

Small chakra: Located under the left armpit. Rhodochrosite, emeralds, and jade are the most commonly used crystals in this chakra. This chakra area can be a potential source of energy loss.

CORRESPONDENCE BETWEEN CRYSTAL AND CHAKRA

HEART CHAKRA

Primary Chakra: Locates in the center of your chest. Aventurine, malachite and jade are the best crystals for this chakra.

HIGHER HEART CHAKRA

Small Chakra: Locates just above the center of the Heart Chakra. Rose quartz and Rhodonite are perfect for this chakra. A mixture of green and pink is ideal for the heart and upper heart chakra to create the emotional basis for cleansing.

NECK CHAKRA

This is a more critical chakra: Located At the base of the throat. Lapis lazuli, sodalite, turquoise, and aquamarine are perfect for this chakra.

CHAKRA OF PAST LIFE

Small chakra: Located just behind the ear. Blue Fluorite, Amazonite, Amber, and Angelite are perfect for this chakra.

THIRD EYE CHAKRA

Large chakra: Located in the middle of the forehead. Amethyst, Iolite, fluorspar, and tanzanite are perfect for this chakra.

SOMA CHAKRA

Small chakra: Located directly above the chakra of the third eye. Amethyst, charoite, solid fluorspar, and amethyst are excellent options for this chakra.

CROWN CHAKRA

Greater Chakra: It's right above your head. Clear quartz, Herkimer diamonds, and white amethyst are perfect for this chakra.

HIGHER CROWN CHAKRA

Etheric Chakra: Just above the crown chakra. Sugilite, Pink Topaz, and Zircon are perfect for this chakra.

CRYSTAL & AURA CORRESPONDENCES

Every human, plant, animal, and almost every living thing has an aura. Your aura is the electromagnetic field that surrounds your body. The atmosphere consists of seven levels, each with its frequency. They are interconnected and affect each other through our emotions, feelings, thoughts, actions, and health, etc. An imbalance in one body leads to an imbalance in the other entity. If we have negativity, problems, stagnant energy, or other problems, they will appear in our aura field before affecting our bodies. They appear in the aura field as leaks, tears, stagnant energy, and signs of vitality. To tackle these areas and problems, we need to know which suitable crystal works best at each level to reach the root of the problem. Crystals, unlike Crystal Healing, are not associated by color but are used at each station for healing properties and attributes. To use a crystal for aura problems, place the crystal on your dominant hand, and perform the most extensive sweep action possible. Use the right crystals and gems for the suitable coating to repair problem areas and eliminate stagnant and harmful energy sources.

AURA ALIGNMENT

It is a condition in the aura field with citrine.

AURA BOOSTER

Use Sugilite to give your aura field a boost of energy.

AURA CLEANSER

Use lapis lazuli to do the necessary cleaning.

AURA PROTECTION

Use Labradorite to protect and mitigate your basic aura needs.

AURA MOOD & OPENING

Improve your mood and release your aura with Rutile Quartz. First Aura Level: This is called the body's aura and indicates the sensation of the fullness. Use Lepidolite or Jasper to clean and repair your first level.

SECOND AURIC LEVEL

This is called your ether aura body and shows feelings about yourself. Use Angelita or RioLita to clean and restore the second level.

THIRD AURIC LEVEL
This is called your rational mind and helps you understand your situation clearly and reasonably. Use Aventurine or Bloodstone to cleanse and heal the third level.

FOURTH AURIC LEVEL
This is known as your astral or emotional body aura. This level deals with our loving interactions with family and friends. Use Peridot or Rose Quartz to purify and restore the fourth level.

FIFTH AURIC LEVEL
This is known as the lower half of the aura. This level works with sacred energy from

your soul and spiritual level. Use Carnelian or Staurolite to clean and restore the fifth level.

SIXTH AURIC LEVEL

This is known as your upper mental aura body and shows the love and spiritual ecstasy of God. Clean and repair the sixth level using phenacite or turquoise.

SEVENTH AURIC LEVEL

This is known as the mental and intuitive body of the aura. This will help us to connect with the heart of God and understand more universal patterns for experiencing silence. Use Celestite or Elestial to cleanse and heal the 7th level.

HOW TO USE CRYSTALS FOR HEALING?

There are many different ways to use crystals for healing. Multiple crystals have applied to various problems and illnesses. I'm not here to tell you that you have to use a particular crystal in a specific way, or it doesn't work. That is not the purpose of this book. I'm here to help you along your journey of spiritual learning and to help you learn some of the best ways to use crystals and the most effective outcomes for a variety of problems. There are several methods to use crystals for healing, so I'm going to tell you a little bit about common uses of gems so that you can learn the basics and apply them to the right crystals for each area of application. However, keep in mind that other crystals that I have described can be used if they do not resonate in the vibration field. The combination of crystals, how they can be used, and how they can be used to make some of these healing methods more effective.

CRYSTAL HEALING, WEARING OR CARRYING YOUR CRYSTAL

Placing a crystal in the energy field is probably the easiest way to use it, but is it always the most effective? It may or may not be. You have crystal energy in your vibrational energy field, but if you don't put it where you need it most, or leave it there for a long enough, you'll only see the symptoms of the disease and not the cause. Don't touch. If you don't always use this particular crystal until the problem is completely gone, you can go back and restart the process.

On the other hand, if this is what you want to do, or if you want constant access to these energies, wearing crystals is beneficial. An obvious method to do this is to carry the crystal in your pocket, carry it in your wallet, put the crystal in a hanging box, or make it a jewelry item. This is modern and effective! When handling crystals this way, be sure to remove and clean the crystals regularly, as they work not only in the energy field but also in the energy field they come into contact with. So, don't forget to clean them up and schedule it, if needed!

HOW TO USE CRYSTALS FOR HEALING CRYSTAL GRIDDING?

The crystal grid is the placement of stones inside or around the body for healing. This also refers to the placement of crystals in a room or area that contains a meditation circle. Placing stones for treatment can be done by placing crystals or gems near the appropriate chakras or where the disease is detected. The stone can be placed directly in this area or within a few inches of space. Remember to use small and light crystals for this, as they tend to spin and roll. There's a reason for this if you put a crystal in the appropriate chakra point and it falls a few times, it means in general, people and crystals do not resonate with the same combination of vibrations, so choose another crystal suitable for this region. This doesn't happen often, but when it happens, check out the healing session and how it happens. Placing a crystal in a room or area is a straightforward process. For the problem at hand, place the jewel in the room where you spend the most time. It can be a living room, a family room, a bedroom, or even a kitchen. Placing the crystal in the room should be done where the gem is not blocked and has access to the full flow of energy vibrations. Therefore, do not hide them under pillows or blankets that are boxed and wrapped in the closet's trunk. They lose access to energy. Placing it in the corner of the room provides the best access for most rooms, but you can access all rooms for all purposes. Therefore, Crystal Healing should guide you to the best place for your room or area, following the local guidelines. Meditation circles are always a fun and easy way for everyone. These are just the rings of crystals and jewels that surround the body during a meditation session. Place them in a circle to create a uniform symbol with them. This symbol has no end or beginning, so energy is always flowing through all the crystals surrounding your energy field. This is the focus of the highest level of energy during the meditation session. Remember to clean and schedule them regularly.

HOW TO USE CRYSTALS FOR HEALING CRYSTAL ELIXIRS?

Crystal Elixir is a water-based solution with its healing properties and crystalline attributes, including the programming or intent behind it, i.e., to aid healing. Charged water can be rubbed on the affected area, fogged, or sprayed in the air for cleaning and for a variety of other purposes. There are many ways to make Crystal Elixir. I have three favorite ways to use them. There are so many different ways to charge and how to make an elixir, so give it a try and see which one is right for you! Because it is a chemical additive, bottled water or spring water is used to make the elixir instead of tap water. Be sure to store the charged crystal elixir water in the refrigerator for up to 7 days.

Immersing the crystal in water will load it directly. Make sure you have cleaned and programmed the appropriate crystal in advance. Pour water into a glass container and gently pour the crystal into the water. Place your crystal in water for the minimum time suggested for that particular elixir. Gently remove the lens, rinse, dry, and store in a specific place. Indirect charging of crystal can be done similarly, but instead of soaking it in water, place it next to a water container. This is an excellent way for crystals that can be toxic if ingested. Crystal Healing Inside the Crystal Charge is a more sophisticated version of the Indirect Charge of the Crystal, but it has found to be effective when making

Elixirs. To do this, you need two glass bowls. Place the programmed clean crystal in the smallest glass container. Then place the smallest gem in a glass bowl. Next, add bottled water or spring water to the most significant glass container. The crystal must not be in physical contact with water but surrounded by water. After a reasonable amount of time, remove the smallest glass container, the diamond, and pour water from the most significant glass container into the storage container.

When you first enter Crystal Healing, it can be confusing due to the many crystals and gems, and their multiple purposes and uses. It's an immeasurable approach, to begin with, tiny and simple crystals. This way, you will not be overwhelmed by all the available types. You need to create your crystal healing kit or bag. We recommend at least two of the same crystals for each of the seven main chakras associated with them, along with other crystals and gems, have taken to the growing spiritual path. There are also individual general healing stones for men, women, children, and pets. That way, in the event of an emergency, you can get at least some of the essential crystals you already have, which is the nearest one to a specific crystal or stone. You don't have to worry about going to a holistic store.

Here are the elemental crystals you can store in your bag or crystal healing kit:

· Practical crystals that heal 30 red crystals

· Red Jasper or Garnet Orange Crystal

· Carnelian or Topaz yellow crystals

· Tiger eye or calcite green crystals

· Aventurine green or emerald blue crystals

· Turquoise or purple/violet lapis lazuli crystals

· Pink amethyst or fluorspar crystals

· Rose Quartz or Rhodonite White / Clear Color Crystal: Clear Quartz Crystal or Moonstone Black Crystal

Onyx or Black Tourmaline

These are just some of the crystals needed in a crystal healing kit or bag, as well as bandages and antibiotic cleaning in first aid kits. Remember here that you can always add multiple sizes and shapes to your crystal kit or bag. There are also some good crystals and gems that are best suited for a particular type of energy, such as male energy, female energy, child energy, animal energy. These are also great to have in hand, especially if you know your crystal healing and regular working with these energies.

SOME OF THE MAIN MALE ENERGY CRYSTALS AND GEMS ARE:

- Amethyst
- Garnet
- Jade
- Rose Quartz
- Smoky Quartz
- Hematite

- Malachite
- Lapis Lazuli

THE PRIMARY FEMININE ENERGY CRYSTALS AND GEMS ARE:

- Amber
- amethyst
- jasper
- rose quartz
- moonstone
- jade
- obsidian
- sodalite.

BASIC CRYSTAL HEALING BAGS, THE BEST ENERGY CRYSTALS AND GEMSTONES FOR KIDS ARE:

- Amethyst
- Apache tears
- carnelian
- light quartz
- rose quartz

- lapis lazuli
- tiger's eyes
- aventurine

SOME OF THE CENTRAL STONES AND CRYSTALS OF ANIMAL ENERGY ARE:

- Amethyst
- rose quartz
- smoky quartz
- light quartz
- turquoise
- calcite
- carnelian
- sodalite

These are high crystals and gemstones that you should have as an addition to your crystal healing kit or bag, primarily when you work with certain types of energy at work. For example, if you know you are passionate about working with animals, have a crystal at hand that will help you balance your life efficiently and quickly. Primary crystal therapy is considered an old masonry. Stones, crystals, and gems place on the body above the chakra points. Each chakra resonates with a specific color, and the chakras line up and mix. The central policy after the demand for quartz healing is that disease occurs when there is an inequality between God's energy and that of humans. Most healers believe that this divine light or power is the primary basis of universal creation. This book serves as a guide to a better understanding of crystal healing. It turns out that everything from the basic principles to the basic facts about crystals is possible. Read and learn how Crystal Healing can dramatically change your life. Everyone is a little confused about crystals work and how they cure it.

Clear Crystal Healing is a typical cure for gems and crystals. Crystals place on a specific area of the body called the "chakra."

Chakra is a Hindu word for spiritual energy. According to various studies, the human body has seven major energy centers. Some healers place crystals of the same color as the individual chakra to develop a stream of energy. Crystals direct a stream of power to that person to balance their life. Generally, they are used to clean people from negative or harmful points that believed to cause serious illness. Eliminating bad mental energy reduces the severity of the physical disease. These crystals are used in spiritual, physical, psychological, and emotional healing too. But crystal healers are not the only professionals to help others. Even professional nurses have learned to use crystals on their patients. There are several ways to heal your body with Crystal Healing. You can get your maximum benefit by holding them when you are very sick or by keeping them in your pouch. This sort of healing can stabilize and heal your whole body.

The practitioner places individual crystals in the chakras of the body to extract unwanted energy and inject the earth's energy and universal healing into the body. Some spiritual counselors and massage therapists use crystals to teach you how this type of healing works. How does Crystal Healing work? No one knows the actual creator of crystal healing. However, this method has been used for centuries. Throughout history, people have used magic stones, gems, and amulets. Healers claim that this crystal treatment is useful, but there is no concrete scientific evidence to support its real healing power. Most crystal healers use transparent quartz because of its color and shape. However, chakras have different colors in different areas so that you can put gems and crystals of a particular color in the same color chakra. These gems have vibrational frequencies that are stimulated by their shapes and involve the individual's global energy field. Crystals can also be used to recondition or strengthen the human mind by conducting vibrational energy. To keep the crystal, it must be covered with table salt or placed in saltwater. Crystal maintenance is essential to protect the crystal from environmental imbalances.

CRYSTAL HEALING AS AN ALTERNATIVE HEALTHCARE

Many people practice crystal healing as an alternative medicine. Following the advice of your doctor or health care professional is essential, but you can also research and learn about different alternative treatments. Another solution is diamond healing. Rejuvenating your brain and body is all of the scales. Consequently, you need to integrate the crystals into your life. The use of gems and crystals in healing is continuously increasing. Others practice it as a conventional occidental antibiotic medication. Most people use crystals to treat various ailments and illnesses, even in the absence of medical research demonstrating the healing properties of crystals. How Crystal Healing Works Crystal Healing's popularity is due to people's belief in ancient customs that involve rocks, gems, and crystals as a way to balance energy. Healers accumulate crystals. This is because crystals are suitable for each person's condition. Healers favor to locate them near or on energy centers and chakras to create balance.

BENEFITS OF CRYSTAL HEALING

Most people use crystals to relieve the symptoms of pain, stress, and illness. Other gems also can treat conditions such as arthritis, insomnia, depression, and anxiety. Some people undergo regular crystal healing sessions with the use of traditional therapies. Some patients reported increased vitality and increased awareness of mental and physical acuity after undergoing crystal healing. There are a variety of crystals that are great for treating sick body parts.

These types of crystals include:

BERYL
This stone cleans the throat and helps improve liver function.

CITRINE
Promotes blood circulation.

EMERALD
Fights insomnia and provides enough sapphire for sleep-this stone can make your skin healthier.

TOPAZ
Helps to eliminate varicose veins.

SODALITE

This stone helps increase the normal blood pressure range. Some argue that they have experienced a feeling of weightlessness as if they lifted off the ground. On the other hand, some people have passed various energy centers in the body where they feel tingling and heat. During the session, some people fall asleep or go into deep meditation. Some patients say they feel better than before. Crystal Healing behaves differently depending on the patient and condition. Some require a single session, and others are recommended weekly crystal healing to relieve pain and stress. However, the usual treatment course lasts up to 3 sessions. The first reference to the use of crystals for medication has been found in Papyrus, Egypt, around 1600 BC. The method of healing has continued with gems for centuries. You can carry a healing crystal in your pocket. These crystals can also be ground into a powder and mixed with the beverage liquid to get the most out of crystal healing, and it is essential to choose the healing crystal that best suits your needs. If you are unfamiliar with this, please contact your doctor.

BELOW ARE VARIOUS HEALING CRYSTALS THAT YOU SHOULD NOT MISS.

AMETHYST

This type of crystal is considered a master healer. It protects and purifies negativity. It also provides a balance between transition states. This stone has a purple color and connects to the heart chakra. However, not all amethysts are purple. It is also found in bluish red color. It is ideal for strengthening the deep spiritual connection between life and your inner self.

CHEVRON AMETHYST

It helps eliminate karmic patterns and improves mental vision and intuition.

AMBER

It is known as the softest stone of various crystals. It has a calming and relaxing effect. This crystalline healing stone has often been used to build a positive tendency while taking the patient's lifeless things seriously. It is also used to increase loyalty in relationships. Crystal healers see this stone as a form of self-healing. It guides the user to the right feeling. Amber is also devoted to calming emotions for post-operative issues.

TIGER EYE

This is a kind of crystal with golden and brown color. It encourages you to be extra careful and focus on what you are doing. Students are often recommended to use this stone. It also helps improve your mental development. Wearing this crystal will also bring you more blessings.

JADE

This type of crystal is known as a mild stone. Like Bernstein, it calms the emotions and maintains the peace of the community. This stone can also convey self-esteem and self-sufficiency. This helps users deal with their situation. In general, jade improves harmony, calmness, and balance through emotional patience. As a healing function, it helps to recover from unnecessary experiences such as unemployment, funerals, and divorces.

MOONSTONE

According to crystal experts, Moonstone has often been associated with improved intuition. Various options are also available. This stone also invites you to personal change and growth. If you are stubborn and impulsive, Moonstone will be a great help. This sky-blue stone increases concentration and prevents distraction.

AQUAMARINE

This stone has found to calm the nervous system and improve the user's mood. Greatest quartz healers consider that aquamarine is more useful for treating toothache, liver damage, sore throat, and stomach problems. Most sailors prefer to wear this stone for protection.

QUARTZ

The transparent crystal is an energy conductor and acts as a transmitter and receiver. Having this stone will protect you from harmful external fluctuations. This crystal renders consistency and can take good care of your well-being. Research shows that there are various types of quartz crystals. Each has its own function. Rose quartz is associated with sensations and desire. Neutral quartz, on the other hand, is supposed to protect the user from negative energy.

FLUORITE

This crystal is effective in treating stress. It can also cure infectious diseases and is ideal for fighting viruses. Fluorite restores the skin and helps heal wounds and ulcers. It also regenerates the mucous membranes of the respiratory tract. Blue fluorspar is considered the best crystal for treating the nose, throat, eye, and ear problems.

On the other hand, green fluorspar is excellent for stomach disorders, infections, and cramps. Purple fluorspar is best for bone marrow and bone disorders. If someone wants to release toxins from his body or keep his liver healthy, it is recommended to use yellow fluorspar.

BLOODTHIRSTY

This type of crystal has used for all blood-related problems in the body. This helps detoxify the blood, kidneys, liver, and spleen. This dark green stone with scattered red dots can also improve blood circulation.

CARNELIAN

Its function is the same as Bloodstone. It detoxifies the liver and blood. This stone also helps relieve back pain, cramps, and arthritis. It also helps relieve allergic symptoms. Using red and orange rocks as pendants or rings also gives you confidence and a great sense.

WHAT IS THE BEST CRYSTAL?

There are different types of healing crystals, so you need to select the appropriate option. Not all crystals are the same. Please consult a professional before using these crystals. Some therapists argue that some gems have a significant effect on the digestive system, while others are essential for reproductive system recovery. No matter what kind of illness you have, there are corresponding healing crystals that adapt to your condition. If you are not aware of this, be sure to read the information above. You can also ask your friends to get what they need and treat their symptoms immediately.

MINERAL VS CRYSTAL

Ever queried what the real difference is between crystals and minerals? Some argue that they are the same. But they are wrong. There is a big difference between the two and knowledge helps to distinguish them. Clear and crystalline minerals are considered one of the most important natural resources in the world. They occur naturally in solid chemicals. They are often formed by several geological processes. Most of them have very different chemical compositions. They are highly ordered atom formations with other physical properties. Minerals range from structurally pure salts to complex silicates. Minerals have many uses, most of them grown or owned. Crystals, on the other hand, are composed of atoms, molecules, and ions that repeatedly spread in all the spatial dimensions. This technique is known as concentration or crystallization. Crystals initially start as liquid particles and solidify. The crystal structure depends on the chemistry of the liquid in which it has formed. Minerals and crystals are not just different in how they have been used.

There are other differences also:

CRYSTAL

Crystals are composed of several natural materials. Gems are classified as cubic, hexagonal, orthorhombic, monoclinic, rhombohedral and tetragonal. They are also believed to have curative properties and have used in multiple relaxation procedures. The crystals are bright in color and have the property of being translucent. Some of them can reflect light in different colors. Depending on their rarity and crystalline structure, some of them are cheap, while others are quite costly.

MINERAL
MINERALS FALL INTO TWO CATEGORIES:
- **NON-SILICATE**
- **SILICATE**

SILICATE MINERALS
Silicate minerals are substances that have the basic units of silicate minerals.

NON-SILICATE
Non-silicates, on the other hand, fall into multiple classes such as sulfides, elements, hydroxides, and carbonates. Silicate-free minerals are scarce compared to different

types. Treating the condition with crystals is not so difficult. However, it does require sufficient time and proper procedures. We hope that you will get the maximum benefit from them if you use these crystals correctly. Most significant gem healers place stones on different parts of the body to improve the patient's soul, mind, and body. You should know how to use these crystals if you intend to help others, your family, or yourself.

Make a list of illnesses and complaints from your health clients. Whenever possible, get the crystals you need to solve these specific problems. Then have the patient lie on a flat surface that is convenient for the patient. Turn off the lights and make sure the environment is quiet. Make sure the patient wears loose and comfortable clothes. Then gently place the crystals on the areas of your body that you feel uncomfortable. For sleep problems, put crystals in your chest for soul and forehead related illnesses. Begin meditation in the room while the crystal has overlaid on the human body. Focus on the patient's disease and the power of the crystal. You also need to invite patients to join in meditation together. It has said that the more mental energy flows through the crystal, the stronger they become. This process is straightforward. We hope that following this process will make your loved one feel healthier after the sitting.

HERE ARE MORE IDEAS TO PRACTICE THESE GEMSTONES FOR HEALING?

HERE ARE THE STEP-BY-STEP PROCEDURES:

STEP 1 Cleaning Procedure Cleaning is a crucial step when it comes to crystal repair. In this process, the crystals try to remove energy disorders that can cause serious illness. The glass must be in contact with the patient. Every week, crystals have placed in direct sunlight. It can clean the crystal energy and recharge. For the first week, Crystals best adjusts the patient's energy field. This is also the period during which the matrix adapts to your energy. Each practitioner has a specific cleaning method. Some prefer to blend white sage smoky glasses until they are clean, while others use holy water to perform an apparent ritual.

STEP 2 The process of harmony and integration of the changes observed in the first step include the patient's emotional, physical, and spiritual presence. In addition to these developments, choosing to undergo this type of healing process has other changes. The purpose after these differences is the toxins that have eliminated from the body.

STEP 3 Stability At this step, the changes have already been accepted by the body.

After that, these changes stabilize the body. A stable body means that the body can withstand pressure and a nervous environment without healing crystals. However, the number of permanent stages has reduced, and healing crystals have worn to restore health.

HOW TO USE CRYSTAL HEALING?
Crystal healing cannot completely cure your medical problems. However, this is a great alternative, especially in an emergency. Crystals allow you to calm down while waiting for your doctor's arrival. The body has powerful methods of over-healing.

IF YOU OPT TO USE THESE GEMS FOR HEALING, COMMIT TO THE FOLLOWING AS YOUR DESIGN:
Choose the gem, crystal, or stone that's best for your health. This is accomplished by seeking the help of an expert or other source.

Clean the crystal if necessary. This helps remove negative energy and vibrations. The best cleaning method is to leave the stones under the full moon for three days and three nights. Place the crystal in a relaxing place, e.g., Kitchen, bathroom, bedroom, etc. You can combine jewelry and a relaxing time. Do more research on crystal healing to find the exact process. If the process is stupid and unpleasant, it is recommended to skip it. Use your crystal as your intuition says, like a lucky charm. You can carry these crystals in your pocket or purse. With distinct data regarding crystal healing, you can solve health problems for yourself and other family members. You can also share your knowledge with friends and family.

If the crystal is to use for a specific purpose, it must be programmed. Intent and focus are the two most important aspects to consider when planning a program for a crystal. This includes healing, chakra activation, and protection. Even if your purpose is your show, you need to know how to get your presentation on your stone. You need to focus when programming the crystal. When programming, you need to make sure your thoughts are consistent with your intended purpose. For example, if you want to avoid negative vibrations from your miserable co-workers, you should use black tourmaline instead of other types of crystals. Programming all kinds of crystals and gems is one way to store energy patterns in stones. The energy patterns programmed into the rock are thoughts, intentions, sounds, colors, uses, emotions, and other vibrations. You can access these vibrations and return the energy to its original purpose.

If you want to program a crystal, these are the best tips you should not miss:

STEP 1 CLEAN THE CRYSTALS

Whatever crystal type and the method you like, it needs to be precise. The crystal first needs to be cleaned as explained above

STEP 2 GRASP THE CRYSTAL
When grabbing the crystal, use your right hand. Don't keep irrelevant thoughts in mind. Start focusing on the intent of effective crystal programming.

STEP 3 FOCUS ON INTENT
During programming, you need to focus on purpose. You can do this by yelling out descriptive words. For example, if you choose to program the crystal to excellent condition, the phrase "good condition" will be spoken over and over. Depending on your choice, you can whisper so that it doesn't get in the way of others.

STEP 4 REPEAT THE INTENT VERBALLY

When repeating the intent, be sure to grasp the crystal. Never leave a crystal while the program is running. You also need to put your hands on the crystal to generate more vibrations.

STEP 5 REPEAT THE STEPS

Repeat the steps as many times as possible. If you feel intuitive that the crystal has gained vibration, slowly open your hands and thank the crystal.

After these steps, the crystal has fully programmed. This method is also used for spheres, tumble-stones, the natural mineral remains, polished crystals, and natural crystals. To program the crystal, simply grab the crystal while asking to download the programming, and the energies will simply come out.

PROGRAMMING METHODS

Crystal programming is done in many ways. If you are not accustomed to these techniques, you need to investigate further.

For a better understanding, these are the different programming methods you should use:

1. MEDITATION BY VISUALIZATION

Meditation is the usual method of programming a crystal. To do this, you must be sitting in a quiet environment. Next, while grasping the stone, think about the ultimate purpose.

2. ENCOURAGING MEDITATION

The procedure is the same as the old one. However, it takes a few turns. If you feel you are in a permanent state of meditation, stay focused and blow on your crystal.

3. **MEDITATION WITH REIKI AND OTHER ENERGY TECHNOLOGIES**

With this method, you can relax and program the crystal. Follow the above procedures until the feeling of energy disappears in your hands. Some people believe that after programming the crystal, it will stay in that state for almost 28 days.

The main question is, how do you know that you need to reprogram the crystal? For example, if you planned a transparent quartz group in your room to generate high vibrations, you might need to reprogram that group a few weeks later. However, if everything is managed in the first week of programming, you may reschedule it in a few weeks.

TIPS AND TECHNIQUES FOR HARDENING ABANDONED CRYSTALS

Use a Rhodonite crystal for five days as close as possible to your heart chakra to mitigate the problem of withdrawal.

ABDOMEN

Lay down and place two smoky quartz crystals, one directly on the side of the stomach and one in the center. Relax and breathe slowly for 20 minutes to relieve pain and pressure.

SCRATCH

Create a carnelian and obsidian gem elixir, charge it for 1 hour, and tap or moisten this area as many times as you need.

RICH

Make an emerald gem elixir, charge it for 24 hours, and gently spray it on any area of your home, office, or wherever you want to be more abundant in your life.

ABUSE PROBLEMS

Sit in an alternating ring of road crocoite, emerald, and rose quartz. Write down on paper whatever you feel about this situation. Let's continue our life in search of understanding and peace. Fill your role on Mother Earth. Then clean the crystals thoroughly.

RECEIVING

Located in the four corners of a room where you spend most of your time, Charoite creates receptive energy in your life.

ATTAINMENT TARGET

Focus on the target while placing the clear crystal with the pointed end directly in front.

ACID REFLUX

Use Bloodstone and Smoky Quartz in the pendant to reduce symptoms. Each night, place both crystals in the heart chakra for 15 minutes to heal the root cause. Clean thoroughly every night! Acne: Make Amethyst Gem Elixir, charge it for 2 hours, and gently apply this water to your face twice a day.

ACTIVE ENERGY PROBLEM

To remedy these issues, carry a red jade for five days in the aura field.

ADHD

Wear a green jade bracelet on your dominant wrist and a black onyx anklet on your opposite ankle to balance the energy in your pinna.

CONFIRMATION MANTRA

Hold Rhodonite in hand when asserting mantras every seven days to improve performance.

POSITIVE

Quickly rub blue tourmaline to charge both ends with positive and negative charges. Then focus the positive lot near the problem or offensive person. The positive energy of peace has dispersed, and you feel calm.

AIRPOWER

Bring or wear blue lace agate to enhance the vibration of air energy for seven days.

AIR CLEANER

Make a clear crystal gem elixir, charge it for 2 hours, and lightly spray it in the air and areas that need purification.

AIRPLANE EAR

For pain and pressure in flight, be sure to use a combination of fluorspar and black tourmaline and turn counterclockwise within 2 inches of your ear until ear pain and stress have reduced.

AKASHIC RECORDS

For easy access to Akashic Records, place five Chinese writing stone crystal grids around you during meditation. Place one in front of your body, one behind, one on each side, and hold the last one in your dominant hand during the session.

ADJUSTMENT

Lie down and place the three citrine crystals around your body. Place one on your foot, one on your abdomen, and one on your crown chakra for 15 minutes.

ALLERGIES

Make a carnelian gem elixir, charge it for 2 hours, and lightly spray it all over your body from head to toe three times a day.

AMPLIFICATION OF CRYSTAL HARDENING

If you use other crystals in your healing session, use phenacite to amplify the healing effect. For best results, combine the crystals used in that particular session with your phenacite with your dominant hand.

ANAL CRACK

Take a relaxing bath with plenty of carnelians and golden topaz. Please bathe for 10 minutes, at least. Repeat as many times as you need.

ANALYTICAL PROBLEMS

Wear a purple crystal for five days to see the difference in energy coordination for this issue.

ANGEL COMMUNICATION

Surround yourself like a little angel during the meditation session and watch the connection improve.

ANGER

Hold the blue lace agate and breathe slowly and deeply. Feel the wrath of Mother Earth and all the violence that is reborn with positive energy. It takes about 5 minutes to calm down and cool down!

ANIMAL COMMUNICATION

If you use animal communication to improve connectivity, be sure to use Fadden Quartz.

ANIMAL INJURY

Take the Rose Quartz and place it within a few inches of the animal's injury. Rotate the crystal clockwise to remove stagnant negative energy from injury. Note adverse reactions from animals, as they cannot integrate crystal energy as fast as humans.

ANIMAL PROTECTION

Attach the Angelite to the animal's crate or collar for extra protection in the energy field.

ANXIETY

Hold the peridot in your dominant hand and rub it lightly with your thumb. You can also place it on your heart chakra and breathe slowly and deeply. Your anxiety level will decrease in minutes.

APPRECIATION

To use it yourself, carry or use the howlite in the energy field for at least three days and make sure to check if the energy changes significantly. To tackle the issue with others, place two people in opposite corners of the room, spending at least 14 days most of the time and observing behavioral changes.

ARGUMENT

Take your hematite and hold it gently in your hand during the discussion. Exhale all breathe slowly and slowly into hematite. Lower your hand, grasp the hematite with your dominant hand, and relax for a few minutes to soothe any problems that arise.

GRAZING PROBLEM

Wear emeralds for seven days to address ego problems and arrogance.

ARTHRITIS

Make Carnelian Gem Elixir, charge for 3 hours, and wash your hands with this water to relieve pain. You can also water the affected area directly.

ASCENSION

During a meditation session, hold small white spirit quartz, one in each hand, to develop your ascension skills.

POSITIVE

If you need to be more proactive to increase vibration levels, such as at work, carry Amazonite with you.

ASTHMA

For those who have asthma, the chain tiger pendant should be low enough to get as close to the lungs as possible. Vibrating energy helps calm the problems you face and reduces attacks.

REMOVING THE ASTRAL POWER CABLE

Use Variscite when working in a heavenly power cord removal session. When pulling the power cord, remember to hold it with your dominant hand and use this vibration level of energy to seal the power cord tightly.

ASTRAL PROJECTION

Add hematite to the circle around you before beginning the session. Or, once the course starts, hold it in your dominant hand!

ASTRAL JOURNEY

Geodes are ideal for working on astral trips and coming in a variety of forms, including quartz, amethyst, citrine, and calcite. To address celestial travel issues, try to be surrounded by as many geodes as possible during your stellar travel session. Make sure they are all from the same crystal. Clear quartz and amethyst are perfect for this purpose.

ATHLETE'S FEET

Soak your feet in water with emeralds and smoky quartz. Be sure to clean up the crystal after each session.

AURA ADJUSTMENT

During the aura session, citrine is incorporated into the healing to balance and align energy with the body.

AURA STAR

Use Sugilite to absorb the negative energy from your aura field. Remember to clean every day before daily use!

AURA CLEANER

During the cleansing session, wear lapis lazuli and walk around the client's aura field to deliver energy, healing tears, holes, stagnant or negative energy. Be sure to clean the crystal after the session.

THE BEGINNING OF THE AURA

Use rutile quartz during your aura session to create a more open and responsive aura field. Autism: Be sure to place charoite around the area where people with autism spend most of their time calming the problems they face inside.

CAR TRIP
Be sure to keep Moonstone in your car's trunk and glove box when traveling. When traveling on a scooter or motorcycle, be sure to keep it in the passenger compartment.

CONSCIOUSNESS
Wear a Celestite pendant and place it in a common area of your home or office. Besides, wear it during your meditation session to free yourself.

BACK ISSUES
For short-term discomfort, lie on your stomach and ask three pieces of petrified wood to rest evenly on your back, from the nape of your neck to your bones of your tail. Sleeping for 15 minutes will relieve back pain. If you always have problems, use an

inverted pendant so that the petrified wood sits on your back for five consecutive days instead of your chest. The severity of the pain diminishes.

BAD BREATH
Make carnelian and onyx gem elixir, charge for 15 minutes, and rinse the oral cavity as needed.

BALANCE OF THE PHYSICAL AND SPIRITUAL WORLD
Take the moldavites at these times and regain the balance between the physical and spiritual worlds.

LOCKER
Onyx is a conventional physical balancer. Attach this to the pendant around your neck to restore balance throughout your body.

PRESSURE ULCER

Make a turquoise and black tourmaline gem elixir, charge it for 20 minutes and soak a cotton ball in the tincture. Using a dipped cotton ball, gently tap the pressure ulcer several times with charged water as needed.

BED WET PROBLEM

Place the gold topaz on the two opposite corners of the bed frame and the carnelian on the other two different edges of the bed frame to solve the bedwetting problem.

BEHAVIORAL ISSUES

For best results with behavioral issues, have the tiger's eye used on the ankle opposite to the dominant hand.

BIPOLAR DISORDER

Use a combination of turquoise, rose quartz, and onyx to balance the bipolar disorder problem. Turquoise and Rose Quartz are best worn around the wrist or hand, and Onyx are best worn around the ankle for a winning combination.

BLADDER PROBLEMS

With the waist down, place two amber Colors, one on each side of the abdomen. Apply energy and rest for 20 minutes.

FLOATING

If swelling occurs, lay three golden topaz on their side and place all three in the shape of a triangle on the stomach/abdomen. Make sure one point near the crown chakra and the other two are under the triangle above this. Take a break and relax for 15 minutes. Repeat as necessary and remember to clean the crystal when the session is over ultimately.

LOCKED ROOT CHAKRA

Hold the Lodestone 4 inches from the root chakra and rotate it clockwise to clear the clog. Don't forget to clean thoroughly afterward.

BLOCKED SACRAL CHAKRA

Place carnelian on each side of the sacral chakra, hold a citrine 4-inch from the chakra, and rotate clockwise to remove the blockage. Don't forget to clean the crystal thoroughly afterward.

LOCKED SOLAR PLEXUS CHAKRA

Place the yellow jasper on both sides of the solar plexus chakra, hold 4-inch clear quartz from the chakra, and rotate clockwise to remove any clogging. Don't forget to clean thoroughly afterward.

LOCKED HEART CHAKRA

Place rose quartz on each side of the heart chakra, hold the moldavite 4 inches from the chakra, and rotate clockwise to clear the blockage. Don't forget to clean the crystal afterward.

LOCKED THROAT CHAKRA
Place the sodalite on either side of the throat chakra and keep the lapis lazuli within 4 inches of hands on crystal healing range, heal 42 inches from the chakra and turn clockwise to clear the blockage. Don't forget to clean thoroughly afterward.

LOCKED THIRD EYE CHAKRA
Place fluorspar on both sides of the third eye chakra, hold a 4-inch Prehnite from the chakra and rotate clockwise to remove any blockages. Don't forget to clean thoroughly afterward.

CROWN CHAKRA ROCK
Hold the dumb light within 4 inches of the crown chakra and rotate clockwise to clear

the clog. Don't forget to clean the crystal thoroughly afterward.

ROCK FEET CHAKRA
Hold the hematite within 4 inches of the root chakra and turn clockwise to clear the blockage. Don't forget to clean thoroughly afterward.

LOCKED HAND CHAKRA
Place amethyst on each side of the hand chakra, hold clear quartz 4 inches from the hand chakra, move your energy, and pull the all-purpose source to clear the blockage. Don't forget to clean thoroughly afterward.

BLOOD CIRCULATION
Wear citrine pendants, bracelets, and anklets to help connect and flow!

BLOOD PRESSURE
Wear a combination of black and green tourmaline always to balance these issues.

BLOODY EYES
Make a clear, emerald quartz elixir, charge for 1 hour, and place a few drops of charged water on each eye. Repeat as needed.

RELEASE
With red jade in both hands, it focuses on the problem occurring within and gives three slow deep breaths. Be sure to wash thoroughly after use.

BODY IMAGE PROBLEMS
For body image issues, wear a smoky quartz necklace and an anklet at the same time to reverse these issues and look in perfect sacred order.

LINK PROBLEM
Place Jade and Rose Quartz in the area opposite the room where the two people spend together. These energies will help them link faster.

BONE

Make Fluorite Gem Elixir, charge it for 24 hours, and gently spray it on the area of bone you want to strengthen. You can also use the water bath to pre-charge the bathwater for 10 minutes to increase vibration levels and improve bone-building capacity.

BONE LOSS

Use Rhodonite 24 hours a day, six days in a row. Then, clean it for a day. Repeat as needed.

LIMIT THE PROBLEM

Be sure to schedule and take Barite to places where boundary problems occur, such as your workplace or relatives' home. Wear this as often as possible when in the area and clean it after each session.

BALL PROBLEM

Use Yellow Jasper in a healing session to calm intestinal issues. Be sure to use three during the session—one on each side of the client, one on the lower abdomen.

EEG

Take a meditation, sleep, or rest with Herkimer Diamonds near your head to improve EEG frequency changes and mental conditions.

BREAKING TIE

Use Onyx to address issues related to tie failures. Wear one on the ankle and one on the dominant wrist for seven days. Don't forget to clean them later!

BROKEN HEART

Use Green Aventurine and Rose Quartz together to repair broken hearts. Lying for 15 minutes, place the two crystals on the heart chakra. When you get up, wrap it in paper and bury it in your backyard for five days. Remember to dig them up after five days and clean gently.

BLUES

Make an elixir of petrified wood and a hematite gem, charge it for 2 hours, and spray or tap it gently on the injured area as needed.

BOMB

Wear a Carnelian and smoky quartz anklet around the ankle to block energy in that area and cure the root cause of the aneurysm.

ROAD

Carry your amber in your pocket or bag to solve your luggage problems. For a more reliable connection, hold it for 24 hours, three days to ultimately reduce the burden.

BURNS

Make chrysoprase elixir, charge the water for 1 hour, and lightly touch the required area with this charged water. You can also add a drop of this to any other remedy, cream, or ointment used for additional healing purposes.

BUSINESS CAREER

Pick up a malachite and focus on the success of your business and what you want to change or bring about. Place malachite near your wallet for the next five days and dream of trading! Soothing: Lie down, wrap yourself in blue topaz and agate for 15 minutes, and feel calm.

CALM DOWN

Lying down, place agate and amethyst on the chakra of the third eye and take a deep breath. After about 10 minutes, you will be calm, relaxed, and fresh.

CANCER

Use selenite in crystal healing sessions for cancer problems. Perform a complete head-to-toe healing session with selenite. Then remember to clean the crystal completely.

CARPAL TUNNEL

Make Blue Lace Agate Gem Elixir, charge for 3 hours, and wash your hands with this water to relieve pain. You can also water the affected area directly.

CELL HEALING

Program and use Eternal Quartz to enhance efficacy during cell healing sessions.

CELLULAR MEMORY

Use Citrine Herkimer to improve cell memory. Whatever your session, be sure to surround it or hold it in your hand.

CELL UPDATE

Take six sticky balls and lie on your back—place two on your feet, one on your crown chakra, and one on your abdomen. Breathe deeply and slowly, absorbing the energy you need for 20 minutes at a time. Repeat until the desired result is visible.

CELLULITE

Make a hematite gemstone and golden topaz elixir, charge it for 1 hour and gently spray it wherever cellulite is visible. Repeat 3 times a day.

CENTRAL

For centering practice, hold the yellow topaz near the solar plexus chakra and the black phantom quartz at your feet. Breathe slowly and deeply for 10 minutes.

BALANCED CHAKRA

To balance the chakras, take seven crystals (one for each chakra with matching colors) and lie on your back. Place the corresponding crystal in the chakra for 20 minutes. Be sure to clean everything individually after the session. To expand your session, surround yourself with four transparent crystals. One on the feet, one on each side of the body, and one on the crown chakra. Make sure the transparent crystal faces inward.

CHAKRA ENERGY FLOW

After the chakra balance session is complete, place an eternal crystal in the crown chakra. Rest, relax, and enjoy a new powerful energy flow for 15 minutes!

OPEN CHAKRA

A closed chakra is opened by placing fluorspar on the chakra while lying down. Turn fluorspar three times clockwise. If the chakra is still closed, repeat another session until it opens and flows naturally.

CHANGE

Use Purple Rainbow Fluorite to help change. Carry it for the time as much as possible in your daily life. Clean it every day during this period.

CHANGE YOUR PERSPECTIVE
Hold a transparent calcite crystal in your dominant hand and focus on the subject for 10 minutes. Take this with you for the next few days and see the changes taking place in your point of view.

CHANNEL CAPACITY
Surround yourself with Sugilites before the session begins or hold them in hand before starting the channeling course. People also sleep with this crystal under their pillows to increase their connection.

CHAOS

Bring the tanzanite closer to the solar plexus chakra and breathe deeper in chaotic situations.

JOY

Put watermelon tourmaline where you spend most of your time and observe changes in attitudes towards a better direction.

CHICKEN

To relieve itching and scratches during chickenpox development, use black tourmaline, carnelian, and gold topaz to make the gem elixir. Charge for 1 hour and gently spray from head to toe as needed.

BIRTH OF A CHILD

Use moonstones to mitigate labor issues by wearing them as pendants or doing this crystal healing practice nearby during the labor process. It will calm you and your baby during this new adventure.

COLD

Make an Aragonite Gem Elixir and charge it for 30 minutes. Remove the crystals and warm the water. Put the clean towel in the water and rinse the excess. Put this on a person's head or neck.

CHRONIC FATIGUE

Use green phantom quartz to address issues related to chronic fatigue. Be sure to clean it once a day before using it.

CLAIRE AUDIENCE

Wear Snowflake Obsidian and place it as close to your ears as possible. They do not help your physical ears but your inner hearing. You can even put it under your pillow, make earrings, or attach it to your headphones when you sleep. The possibilities are endless!

PERSPECTIVE

Use Hawk's eyes in meditation and channeling sessions to boost mental development. You can surround yourself with those rings, hold them in your dominant hand, or wear them on a pendant to enhance and achieve your natural see-through ability.

CLARITY

Rainforest Jasper has a tremendous effect on this field. Tell Rainforest Jasper about issues that are confusing and need to be clarified. Take this with you in case of confusion. Within a few days, usually a few hours, the excitement disappears, and clarity is restored.

CLEAN CARPET TOXINS

Be sure to place malachite in the four corners of the room to remove toxins from the carpet. Clean the malachite after seven days.

CLEANING BODY

Lie down and place five yellow jasper around your body, one on the crown chakra, one on each side of the body, one on foot, and one on the abdomen. Relax and take a deep breath for 15 minutes.

CLEAR

Sit in a chair and have someone pick up a topaz crystal and use it to move the aura layer and the energy field slowly. Once this has done, cleanse the Topaz.

CLUMSINESS

Using copper is an effective way to eliminate awkwardness. You can see that the copper bracelet and anklet work best. However, incorporating a copper chain necklace into a clear quartz pendant still works amazingly.

COLIC

For colic problems, keep Rhodonite within 2 inches of the baby's midsection and rotate it clockwise three times every 5 minutes to resolve energy fields and colic behavior.

COLD SORE

Make a carnelian and turquoise gem elixir, charge it for 1 hour and soak a cotton ball in the tincture. Use a cotton ball soaked in water to tap herpes gently. Use a fresh and clean cotton ball for each application.

COMMON COLD

For a common cold, use Yellow Topaz to relieve symptoms. You can use this crystal to charge your bath water for 10 minutes before relaxing in the warm bath. You can also lie down and place this crystal around your head, establishing the first one on top of the third chakra to dehydrate excess water.

COMFORT

When you need comforting energy, grab gold calcite, and concentrate. Crystals can pull stagnant energy and release it into space, where you can see things in a new light with comfortable energy.

COMMUNICATION

Wear the aquamarine as a pendant as close to your throat chakra as you can to restore full balance to help with communication problems.

COMMUNICATION WITH PLANTS/ANIMALS

Find the plants and animals you want to communicate with and bring the fairy crystal to your dominant hand. Ask the question you want to know and wait for the answer. Answers can manifest as emotions, messages, words, thoughts, images, signs, so keep your possibilities open.

COMPASSION

Create an Ajoite Elixir, charge it for 2 hours, and fog a caring area, whether it's your home or office, and watch the change emerges

CONCENTRATION

Bring or wear blue topaz on your body to improve your strength. If you're studying in a specific room at home, make a blue topaz elixir, charge it for 1 hour, and atomize that place.

CONSIDERATION

When faced with concussion problems or symptoms, place the hematite directly on the crown chakra, one in one hand and one in the other foot chakra. Make someone have clear quartz within an inch and turn it every 5 minutes clockwise until symptoms subside.

RELIABILITY

Carry or wear Eudialyte for even more confidence. Program this before wearing to maintain vibration levels.

CONFLICT
Place the citrine spirit quartz in the location of the vibration problem and on the opposite corner of the area for the best results.

CONFUSION
Place Peridot in front of your heart chakra and focus on the issue that is currently confusing to see the solution. Repeat for a short time frame that lasts only 5 minutes at a time.

CONGESTION
Lying down, place Aventurine on your lungs and breathe slowly for 10 minutes. Wash the crystal and repeat as often as necessary.

CONNECTION (PAST AND FUTURE)
When working in a session, use the blue apatite on your dominant arm and the purple apatite on the other side to manipulate past and future connections.

CONSTIPATION

Lay down and place three Ajoite around your body, one on each side of your lower abdomen and one in the middle. Relax for 15 minutes and let the energy flow.

CONTENT

Carry or wear Halite to address satisfaction issues. Remember to cleanse after seven days.

ADJUSTMENT

Using fluorspar, put this in your pocket to solve the adjustment problem. If you do this for at least five consecutive days, you will notice a change in the adjustment.

CORN

Soak your feet in a black onyx gem elixir that surrounds your entire foot. Make a ring around your feet, immersing at least six crystals per foot for 15 minutes at a time.

COUGH

Lying down, place two sodalites on each side of the neck, yellow jasper in the chest area, and one clear quartz crystal on the throat chakra to relax and breathe slowly. You can also make gem elixirs with these crystals. Charge for 1 hour, then put three drops under the tongue when coughing begins.

VALUE

Create an aquamarine and carnelian elixir, charge it for 6 hours, and spray it on the most productive areas.

OBSTACLE

Lying down, place two bloodstones, one on each side of the area, and set clear quartz on the entire region. Relax and breathe. Be sure to clean up the crystal after each session.

CREATIVITY

Surround yourself with an amethyst that can be anywhere. The more you have, the more vibrating energy will flow for your creativity. Now you can meditate, place it throughout your home or office, and even spray a charged amethyst mist onto the area you're working on.

CRISIS

Wear or use Rose Quartz during critical times. You can also recharge your bath water with Rose Quartz and exalt these problems with a warm and relaxing bath.

CROHN'S DISEASE

To relieve the symptoms, always lie down and place two clear quartzes on each side of the lower abdomen, with the smoky quartz on the navel. Relax 15 times three times a day to alleviate symptoms.

CROSSOVER

When faced with death, enclose the area as much as possible with Chiastolitic, also known as Cross stone, to help the souls cross. You can also use it if you have a lost Earth soul who needs the help of passing in one session to release a bond trapped in Earth.

CRYING

Place the rose quartz on the heart chakra and the smoky quartz on both sides of the body. Relax, cry, and release any stored energy. Clean the crystal after each session.

DANDRUFF

Make Snowflake green jade and obsidian gem elixir and charge for 1 hour. After washing and rinsing the hair, gently spray this charged water over the entire scalp and let it air dry for the best results.

DENY

Bring your Elestial Quartz or use it for seven days on denial related issues.

RELIABLE

Put black onyx in each pocket to enhance energy vibration and reliability. If there is a problem with the location of others, make an elixir, charge it for 2 hours, and gently spray all areas related to them.

DEPRESSION

Carry it in your pocket or use it as a pendant and wear smoky quartz to deal with depression problems.

DERMATITIS: Make an elixir with gold topaz and lapis lazuli gems, charge for 1 hour, and gently spray on all affected areas. Repeat as needed.

DESPAIR

Combining Green Ghost Quartz and Rose Quartz can tackle the problem of despair. Charge, schedule, and clean daily before use.

DEDICATION

If you are focusing on issues related to the commitment, put a diamond grid formatted garnet in the middle and wrap yourself up for 30 minutes a day. Do this for seven consecutive days, at approximately the same time each day.

DIAPER RASH

Make a turquoise and clear crystal gem elixir and charge for 1 hour. Add a few drops of this electrically charged water to a cream or ointment applied to the baby's hips to cure the rash much faster.

DIARRHEA

Place a transparent crystal near the center of your pocket or belt to soothe the healing vibrations.

DIFFICULTY SWALLOWING
Lying down, place lapis lazuli on both sides of the throat chakra. There is clear quartz in the throat chakra and fluorspar in the third chakra. Take a break and relax for 15 minutes. Thoroughly clean the crystals, make an elixir with a jeweler, charge for 1 hour, put a few drops under the tongue several times a day.

DIGESTION
Put jasper in your pocket for seven days from morning to night and watch your digestive problems go away.

ADDRESS OF LIFE

During this time, please bring white jade as much as possible. You can make Jewel Elixirs, charge for 30 minutes, and gently spray where you are most often.

COMMAND ENERGY
Place a topaz crystal at the top of the situation using a proxy, such as a person's letter or photo. If this is related to your work problem, place it around the office or on top of files. Do this for at least five days, and remember to clean the crystal later.

OBSTACLE
Place amethyst and carnelian around people or homes where you spend most of your time. This helps calm the energy associated with the disorder. Be sure to clean it once a week.

DISCONNECT FROM HIGHER BEINGS

Dress up in a circular transparent selenite during meditation to improve your connection.

HEALING DISTANCE
To enhance your remote healing session, combine cobalt and clear quartz during healing.

MAREO
Make sure you have a transparent quartz point pendant and wear it to focus your energy during dizziness.

DNA ACTIVATION
During the DNA activation session, wear leopard crystal to increase effectiveness. Surround yourself or hold it in your dominant hand during the session.

DOUBT

Carry the Staurolite in your pocket or use it on a pendant for maximum effectiveness at these times. Be sure to clean after use. Dominant energy to focus on your life and become more assertive, attract more dominant power, and be sure to put Apache tears in each pocket, so you don't get hit.

DRAW NEGATIVE ENERGY

Gripping the jet with a dominant hand during denial draws power. Focus on what's positive and sort this out after the session.

SLEEP STIMULATION

If you want to dream more at night, place citrine under your pillow before going to bed. Your subconscious expresses your life through the state of your dreams!

SLEEP MEMORY

If you already have goals but need help remembering them, place Herkimer diamonds under the pillow before going to bed. This stimulates morning memory!

DRY EYES

Lying down, place aquamarine on each eye, and a clear crystal on top of the third chakra for 10 minutes. Repeat as needed.

DRY MOUTH

Make a lapis lazuli and turquoise gem elixir, charge it for 30 minutes and rinse it with water as much as you need.

DYSLEXIA

To tackle the dyslexia problem, have a person carry or use as much Scapolite as possible for the best results.

EAR PAIN
With your back lying, place amber pieces on each side of your head, next to your ears. Relax and rest for 20 minutes to relieve pain.

EARTH ENERGY
Pick up the Brown Jade, preferably barefoot outside, and return to Mother Earth. It also uses this crystal around the ankle to draw more power from the earth.

ECZEMA
Create an Ocean Jasper Gem Elixir, charge it for 1 hour and gently spray or pat as needed. Repeat as many times as you need.

EFFICIENCY
For efficiency issues, carry or use Limonite for seven days as much as possible.

ELECTROMAGNETIC PROBLEM

Take two hand stones (one in each hand) and balance them around the palm chakra for 15 minutes to address electromagnetic issues. Don't forget to clean up the crystal later.

LOCKED EMOTIONS

Use a combination of green tourmaline and rose quartz to release blocked emotions completely. Lie down and place these crystals in your heart chakra for 15 minutes at a time. Repeat this every day until they are entirely free. Depending on the lock, it can take a total of 1-14 days.

EMOTIONS TO CALM DOWN

Wear moonstone if emotions dominate. This helps calm you down very quickly. Don't forget to clean up the crystal later.

EMPATHY

If necessary, lie down and place the pink beryl on the heart chakra to focus on the subject in front of you. Relax and take a deep breath. Don't forget to concentrate during this time.

EMPHYSEMA

Create a chrysotile gem elixir, charge it for 2 hours, and slowly spray it on every area of your home, office, or car every 48 hours for ten days, creating a healthier environment. For the body, lie down and place the chrysotile on the chest, with two clear crystals facing up, one on each side of the body, and rest for 15 minutes at a time. Repeat as many times as you need.

RESISTANCE

For endurance issues, carry it in your pocket or attach it to a pendant and use sodalite and bloodstone. The combination increases durability when required.

ENERGY CONNECTION

If you want to establish a closer relationship with a person, especially if you're going to make an energetic connection, wear garnet for three days and place the garnet on another person's third-eye chakra to make a connection.

ENERGY INCREASE

Sit in a chair with two clear crystals, one in each hand and your feet on the floor. Make sure the pointed end is facing you. Breathe slowly and deeply for 10 minutes to boost your energy quickly.

ENERGY BALANCE

When balancing your energy, use two larimar crystals, one in each hand, and sit comfortably in your chair. Relax and absorb vibrational energy through the hand chakra for 10 minutes.

ENERGY FLOW

Place part-time jobs on one chakra at a time. Start with the crown chakra and proceed to the first chakra. Then do the opposite, working from the root chakra to the crown chakra. Place a part-time job in the chakra area for 3 minutes per chakra to increase energy flow.

CLEANING OF ENERGY NETWORKS

While cleaning the grid, surround yourself with an ammonite, or it in your hold your dominant hand to improve results.

ENERGY PRINTING WASTE

For best results during an energy fingerprint removal session, wear Sherman Phantom Quartz. Always wear a Sherman Phantom Quartz on your dominant hand when performing a power impression elimination session.

ENERGY VAMPIRE
For added protection from energy vampires, always wear amber as a pendant and anklet.

ENTHUSIASM
Wear or carry your Fire Agate and watch your energy levels change and excitement increase in minutes!

ENTITY RELEASE WORK
To complement the entity's release session, place Charoite around the client. If the course has conducted remotely, enclose the practitioner and client.

EQUALITY
Make Morganite Elixir, charge it for 1 hour and gently spray it on all areas of your home

or office to solve your equality problem. Repeat twice a week.

BALANCE
To solve the balance problem, lie down and place China on the crown chakra for 15 minutes.

EXHAUSTION
When you're exhausted, put on Cooper's necklace, bracelet, and anklet. This additional energy boost gets you out of this vibration state. To reinforce this, attach a transparent crystal to either.

FORMULA
Wear the turquoise on a very short pendant as close as possible to the throat chakra and watch as your emotions, feelings, and expressions begin to spread!

EXTERNAL NEGATIVITY

Use sodalite to block and repair adverse external problems when using or shipping it in the aura field. It can also be a computer located to reduce EMF damage.

EYES (GENERAL QUESTION)

For eye problems, make sure you have three amethyst crystals and one turquoise crystal. Lie down and place the turquoise on the third chakra. The three amethyst need to be put in the crown chakra, one on each side of the head, aligned with the eyes. Make sure the amethyst is facing your charge. Take a 20-minute break and relax.

EYE (SCRATCH ON THE CORNEA)

Lying with closed eyes, place Celestite on the injured eye, and rest for 10 minutes. Then place the crystal within 2 inches of the eye and rotate it more than five times clockwise to relieve pain and inflammation and accelerate the healing process.

SYNCOPE

If you tend to faint, wear fluorite on your pendant and turquoise on your bracelet as much as possible to reduce the severity and occurrence of fainting spells.

KINGDOM FAIRY ENERGY

Use fairy crystals in your garden or backyard area to improve your connection with fairy energy. You can also make a gem elixir, charge it for 1 hour, and lightly spray it on the external and internal areas where you want a stronger bond with these energies.

JUSTICE

Make clear quartz, rose quartz and tree agate gem elixirs, charge for 1 hour and gently spray on those who need only energy or the area.

FAITH

Wear or use a combination of emeralds and clear quartz to refocus and believe and remind you to stay in the light of faith!

FAKE IMAGE

Wear or use Charoite during difficult times to see if the rejection problem goes away. That way, you can be more willing to be yourself.

FAMILY ISSUES

Deal with family problems by bringing or using rainforest jasper. You can even make a gem elixir, charge it for an hour and spray it around the home where your family spends most of their time.

FANTASY (CREATE)

Put Ulexite in your pocket and create a fantasy lifestyle that expresses your creativity.

FANTASY (REDUCTION)

Be sure to use obsidian around your throat chakra to reduce fantasy issues and escape.

FATIGUE

To combat fatigue, wear an Onyx anklet and a clear crystal pendant to change the vibration pattern.

FEAR

Use Agate in the long hanging chains near the heart chakra and get the maximum benefit when dealing with fear problems!

LEG

For pain or leg pain, place sea salt, four black tourmalines, and one hematite in a bathtub with warm water. Place the hematite near the top of the toe, two black tourmalines on each side of the foot, and two other black tourmalines behind the heel. Soak your feet for 15 minutes. Be sure to clean after use.

WOMEN'S ENERGY BALANCE

Make a pink tourmaline gem elixir, charge it for 2 hours and spray it lightly throughout your home or office, especially in the corners.

CONCEPTION PROBLEM

Carnelian has best used for infertility, impotence, and menstrual problems. For men or women, carry this for at least seven consecutive days to maximize vibration healing energy. If you have issues with fertility, place carnelians in all four corners of the room to stabilize your life there.

FEVER

Make an agate gem elixir, charge it for 20 minutes, and every 20 minutes lightly spray a person's crown chakra, hand chakra, and foot chakra to lower the heat. You can also place it on a person's sideways on the crown chakra and hematite on the limbs for a more substantial effect.

FIBROMYALGIA

Use Tan zine Aura Quartz to address fibromyalgia problems. You can also make a gem elixir, charge it for 2 hours and use this charged water to gently rub your muscles and joints, or even apply lotion for these ailments.

FINANCIAL ISSUES

The combination of pyrite and green tourmaline is an excellent way to create and discover rich sources. Be sure to carry or use it together. You can also put more energy into your wallet or next to your purse or checkbook.

FIRE ENERGY

To strengthen your connection with the energy of fire, be sure to keep the fire grate in your pocket!

FLATULENCE

Flatulence can be an annoying problem for everyone, so if this becomes more frequent in your life, smoky pocket quartz is used to relieve it the time it occurs. To solve this problem, lie down and place two smoky quartz, one on each side of my lower abdomen. Next, place the gold topaz on the navel and the two hematite at your feet. For best results, rest and relax every 15 minutes a day.

FLORAL ENERGY
Attach a fairy cross around your ankle and connect with the energy of the flowers!

FLU
Use Rainforest Jasper to relieve flu symptoms. During this time, wear it as a pendant around your neck for as long as possible.

LIQUID RETENTION

Place a rainbow moonstone around the liquid holding area. In the case of an injured area, place it above the field and enclose the field as much as possible. Relax and allow the vibrational energy to work for 15 minutes at a time.

FLIGHT / STRESS ISSUES
Put on your hematite pendant and enjoy a flight while calming your nerves and frustration.

WASHING FOOD
Hold the finished clear crystal in your dominant hand and slowly rotate it clockwise three times to remove toxins before eating. Clean after each use.

FORGOTTEN / MEMORY
Carry the emerald and howlite combination with you or put it in your home or office together for the strongest effect. Make sure

you have this as close to you as you can, as this helps recover your memory problems.

FORGIVENESS

Use Sugilite, focusing on having this in your hand and allowing to let go of the problem. I hope all your ties and issues are released, and forgiveness has appeared. Repeat as many times as necessary to remove all connections!

FRIENDSHIP

Use the combination of Moonstone and Rose Quartz for friendship issues. Wear them or take them with you and attract your friends, so be open to anyone who appears in your life.

FRUSTRATION

Take off with the Moss Agate and let go of the frustration of life. It gives you calm, relaxing energy. Hold it with both hands and stand barefoot on the grass. Close your eyes, take a deep breath, and relax. Enjoy all the sound and energy you get for 15 minutes!

GALL BLADDER

Lying on the stomach, place the hematite in the center of the waist and the hematite on foot. Then place two clear crystals, one on each side of the midsection, and relax for 15 minutes to alleviate the gallbladder problem.

GENDER CONFUSION

Carry or use Golden Enhydro Herkimer as much as possible to combat gender confusion.

GENERAL HEALING

Turquoise is a great general healer. It can be used or carried if additional healing energy is needed. Also, lie in a place surrounded by turquoise for 15 minutes, and feel the new energy flows into your body, which is healing you.

GENEROSITY

Generosity begins with a small Jade at home. Carry it in your pocket for at least seven days to get the full effect. You can charge it for 6 hours to make Jade Gem Elixir and lightly spray it around your home once a day for seven days.

GINGIVITIS

Make clear quartz and topaz gem elixir, charge for 30 minutes, and rinse orally with charged water three times a day.

GLAUCOMA

Lying down, place the Tianjin Aura Quartz on both eyes and the Clear Quartz Crystal facing up on the third chakra for 15 minutes at a time.

GOOD FORTUNE
Wear Bloodstone for five days and see how good luck begins!

GRATITUDE
Cobalt is excellent for appreciation issues! Wear it as a bracelet or carry it in your dominant arm pocket.

PAIN
During mourning, carry Apache tears in a bag. You can also lie down and surround your body for a more intense session.

EARTH
To solve the grounding problem, use black tourmaline as an ankle. Wear it for more than 6 hours a day to help energy enter Mother Earth and land ultimately! For best results, wear anklets on each ankle.

TEAMWORK
Place two white spirit quartz in opposite corners of the room to work in a group work session.

GUARD ANGEL CONNECTION
Surround yourself with petalite during your meditation session, even if you are resting and relaxing. Remember to pay attention to the signs that start appearing stronger in your life.

BLAME
Wear or use a combination of leopard skin jasper and rose quartz for seven days to relieve guilt. Don't forget to clean thoroughly afterward.

DINNER
If your gums are inflamed, place mahogany obsidian in the water in a small bowl for 15 minutes. Remove the crystal and gently rub

charged water on the problem area. You can also use it as a mouthwash.

HABIT PROBLEMS

You can wear or carry golden obsidian according to your habits. Making a golden obsidian gem elixir, charging it for an hour, and discoloring all the areas you use most often is a great way to spread this vibrational energy. The Golden Obsidian can also be placed in every corner of the room where you spend the most time.

HAIR GROWTH

Make a snowflake and obsidian gem elixir, charge it for 2 hours, rinse your hair with this charging water or moisten if needed.

HALLUCINATION

Lying down, place the Ocean Jasper on your eyes, and rub your soles for 20 minutes at a time. Be sure to clean up the crystal when you've done it.

HAND PAIN

Make a Carnelian and transparent crystal gem Elixir and charge it for 2 hours. Gently spray your hands or soak in this charged water.

HAPPINESS

Malachite and Rose Quartz have combined the beginning of the wave of pleasure! Wear it on a chain or pendant, as close to the heart chakra as possible.

HARMONY

Milky Quartz is a rich source of vibration that produces pleasant emotions. Put one in every room of the house and clean once every seven days.

HAY FEVER

For hay fever problems, use citrine as much as possible with the pendant. You can also use citrine to charge for 30 minutes to create a gem elixir that gently moisturizes your body from head to toe.

HEADACHE

If you have a problem, take three amethyst crystals and lie down. Place one on each side of the head and the other in the crown chakra, all facing up. When your headache subsides, rest and relax!

HEALTHY HAIR

To make your hair bright and healthy, make Mica Gem Elixir, charge it for 30 minutes, then rinse your hair with this charged water.

LISTEN

Hearing loss can be resolved by combining agate and Rhodonite. When resting, place on either side of the head so that the vibrational healing energies do their work. You can even place it under your pillow when you sleep to absorb the power at night!

HEART
Lie down and place Bloodstone and Rose Quartz on the heart chakra for 15 minutes to relieve heart problems.

ACIDITY
Lying down, put a transparent crystal on either side of the chest, one on top of the crown chakra. Then place the rose quartz on the heart chakra and the citrine on the solar plexus chakra. Relax for 15 minutes.

RASH
Make elixir of fluorspar and amethyst gem, soak it in cold water for 30 minutes and gently spray onto the affected area.

THE ENERGY OF THE SKY

Wear Celestite during your meditation or channeling session and sleep, placing it under your pillow to improve your energy connection.

HEEL SPAR
Lying on the stomach, hematite on the heel spur and carnelian on the back of the knee for 15 minutes, three times a day to relieve pain and symptoms.

HEMORRHOIDS
Place Bloodstone in your pocket to relieve pain and inflammation from hemorrhoids.

HERPES
For an outbreak, lie down and place the fluorspar on the side of the lower back and a clear crystal on the navel. Breathe slowly and slowly. This vibrational healing should be performed once a day for three consecutive days.

HICCUP

For hiccups, make amethyst and lapis lazuli gem elixirs, charge for 5 minutes, then rinse with charged water. Repeat every minute until the hiccups subside.

HIDDEN PROBLEM

When working in a healing or meditation session, use Apache tears to circle a person and hold them with both hands.

MAXIMUM SPIRITUAL CONNECTION

During meditation, wrap yourself around Elestial Quartz and Herkimer Diamonds and use them alternatingly for a more effective high spirit connection session.

ULCER

With your body on the side, cover your body in a clear crystal clockwise and hold the amber part over one hive. Rotate it three times counterclockwise to advance to the next hive area. Continue until you have achieved the healing vibrations.

HOME PROTECTION

Make sure all rooms in your house have clear quartz and black obsidian. Clean and recharge them to protect them and place them in the opposite corner of each room. Remember to clean them every month!

HONESTY

Carrying or using Amazonite for five days will change your attitude, feelings, and thoughts about ethical problems.

HOPE

Combine Amazonite and Aqua Aura to address your desired issue. Best done in 5 days. Be sure to clean up the crystal when you've done it.

HORMONAL CHANGES / PMS / MENOPAUSE

For hormonal issues, especially for women, use green fluorspar to help during these difficult times. Place this crystal in a full spray bottle for 2 hours and gently spray from head to toe once a day to balance these changes. Do not use moonstone, as this crystal aggravates hormonal changes!

HOSTILITY
Carrying and using Ajoite anywhere in your body, not in your wallet, brings stress and all the associated negative emotions to a calm, peaceful silence.

HOUSE CLEANING
Use marcasite during house cleaning sessions to improve the capacity and energy of work.

HUMANITARIAN ENERGY

Use apatite around the throat, chakra to produce more good energy in the aura field.

HUMILITY

Kunzite can help by simply putting this in the aura field for 20 minutes a day. You can lie down, rest with it, and meditate. Keep the options open!

HUMOR

To add more humor in your life and situation, take the fluorspar with you for this purpose programmed for seven days.

HANGER

Wear apatite around your neck to address hunger problems on an empty stomach.

HYPER

Wear hematite around your left ankle to soothe nervous energy.

HYPERSENSITIVITY

It is best to combine Aventurine and Rose Quartz for hypersensitivity! The combination helps healing and comfort at the same time. Wear or use these crystals for three days to experience the full effect.

HYSTERIA

Place the marcasite in the problem area and bring it to the energy field to silence the hysteria problem.

IDEAL

Idealism can work in Bloodstone! This is a simple process of focusing on intent, leaving it on your dominant hand for 15 minutes a day, five consecutive days. Keep this with you for the rest of the time, or wherever you spend most of your time!

LIGHTING CURING

Use Sherman Ghost Quartz during your illuminated healing session to improve your session's skill and strength.

IMAGINATION

After a 20-minute relaxation with Clear Calcite, begin your brainstorming session. Get everything you're working on pencils, sketchpads, laptops, projects, and more. Remember your clear calcite during this time to keep your imaginative juice flowing.

IMMUNE SYSTEM

To boost immunity and stay healthy, try wearing blue quartz around your neck surrounded by chains and copper cords.

IMPATIENCE

Combine amethyst and blue lace agate for more than seven days to improve your patience with minimal discomfort.

INDIGESTION

Sit in a comfortable chair, lay your feet flat on the floor, place your citrine crystal on your sacral chakra with your dominant hand, and the clear crystal with your opposite side on the solar plexus chakra for 10 minutes. Relax and clean the crystals after each use.

INFLAMMATION

For inflammation problems, use Blue Race Agate to relieve these symptoms. Hold it over the affected area and turn the crystal clockwise to extract the stagnant negative energy that causes inflammation. Do this twice a day for 10 minutes until the problem is under control!

ISSUES AFFECTING

When tackling the issue of influence, use Rose Quartz to calm, refocus, and orient everything. During this time, please carry this in your body.

INTERNAL ADJUSTMENT
Surround yourself or hold Faden Quartz with your dominant hand during a meditation session to enhance internal coordination.

CHILD PROBLEM
To increase the effectiveness of your Inner Child Healing session, use Lord Crocite to stay focused on your intentions before starting the course. Keep it at hand during your energy, healing, and therapy sessions to make more effective progress.

INNER EAR
Lie down with four Rhodonite stones, one on the throat chakra, one on the sides of the head at ear level, the last one on the third eye chakra. Rest for 20 minutes at a time and relax to resolve inner ear problems.

INNER PEACE

Please try using Chrysocolla. It is believed to calm and soothe the mind chakra and is useful in solving the problems of world peace. Wear a long chain of copper coating around your neck, as close as possible to your heart chakra.

INSECT BITES

Use Citrine and Clear Quartz Gem Elixir for itching, stinging, and burning on insect bites. Charge the elixir for 1 hour and gently spray onto the affected area as often as necessary. Air dry for best results.

INSECT

Make a little angel jewel elixir, charge it for 30 minutes, and gently spray it on all areas that are in the way of insects, like plants or your home or office.

SAFETY

To relieve anxiety, use Road Crocoite around the neck as close as possible to the heart chakra. You can also soak in a bath loaded with road microsite to mitigate these problems in the aura field.

YOUR PERSPECTIVE

Wear your tiger's eye necklace, bracelet, and anklet to learn about your true self. Start to realize that the answer appears out of nowhere! Use all three for best results!

INSOMNIA

If you have insomnia, place amethyst under your pillow before going to bed so that it is facing up. With a twist or a massive turn, while sleeping, you can even make a crystal bag and sew it on your pillowcase or place it under your head side of the bed. Again, make sure you're looking up.

INSPIRATION

Bring your tourmaline with yourself or put it where you spend most of your time looking for inspiration.

INSTINCT
Use lapis lazuli on your dominant hand or wrist and on the opposite ankle to harness and trust your instincts.

INTELLIGENCE
Combine Jade, Rose Quartz and Lapis Lazuli for the best results when looking for a quick boost. Always carry it in your bag. You can also envelop yourself with them during the breaks and get a little more excited!

INTERCONNECTION
Wear or use the combination of yellow and orange jade that has scheduled for interconnection for seven days. Don't forget to clean up the crystal later.

PRIVACY

For privacy issues, be sure to use lavender jade or place it in all four corners of the room for the best results.

INTUITION

Choose a combination of moss agate and malachite to enhance your intuition. Combined, you can create a conscious balance on both sides of your brain. Carry them in a bag or meditate around your body, alternating between both crystals.

INTUITIVE DREAM

Before going to bed, combine amethyst and jade under the pillow. It is good to put it in a glass bag and secure it to the cushion. This combination creates amazing vibrational energy for intuitive dreams!

INTOLERANCE

Use Rhodonite when dealing with intolerance of friends, family, or even strangers. I don't know when these problems will appear, so this is an excellent crystal to keep in your pocket or purse.

INTROSPECTION
Meditate on the obsidian circle that surrounds your body for introspection issues.

IRRITABLE CUP
Lay down and place Halite on both sides of the hip area and hematite on the lower abdominal site for 15 minutes at a time.

MANDIBLE PAIN
For jaw pain, we use a combination of two different crystals, fluorspar and rose quartz. First, hold the fluorspar, work clockwise, and rotate the crystal around the chin line. Repeat with rose quartz. Other two crystals three times each. You can also make a gem

elixir, charge it for 2 hours, and rub the charged water gently on the outer jaw to relieve discomfort.

CEROS
Bring or use Eudia Light to save the green monster.

TIME COMPENSATION
If jet lag occurs, Marasquita is effective. Hang it on your neck with a pendant or chain and absorb the effect for 1 hour.

JOINT PAIN
For joint pain problems, place azurite on the affected joint for 15 minutes at a time. If you have multiple joint pain problems, put the water which had the crystal for 20 minutes, in the spray bottle, then lightly spray the area and let it air dry. You can also use this charged water by adding a few drops to any cream or ointment you use.

TRAVEL

Surround yourself with crystals of Indicolite Quartz and Hematite alternatively to enhance the experience of your travel session.

JUSTICE / LEGAL MATTERS

When dealing with legal matters, carry or use Jade.

KARMA HEALING

Use Blue Fluorite to improve your karma healing session or your karma problems. Use this during your meditation session, wrap yourself around, or hold it in your dominant hand during the session. Don't forget to clean the crystal later!

KARMA MATRIX HEALING

Use rutile quartz during the Karmic Matrix Healing session for more effective results.

KIDNEY PROBLEMS
Use Smoky Quartz and Yellow Topaz to alleviate kidney-related problems. To relieve these symptoms, lie on the stomach and ask someone to put yellow topaz and the smoky quartz on both sides of the kidney area and the solar plexus chakra.

KINDNESS
Wear Chrysoprase on the pendant for seven days and observe the change in attitude for even more positive results!

KUNDALINI ENERGY
Use Ammonite in a meditation session to boost Kundalini energy. You can also use it during energy or healing sessions. Please hold this in your hand.

LARYNGITIS
Make transparent quartz, lapis lazuli, smoky quartz gem elixir, and charge for 1 hour.

Gargle the charged water as many times as you need. After rinsing, lie down and place clear quartz faced upward on the third chakra, lapis lazuli on the throat chakra, and smoky quartz on the solar plexus chakra for 15 minutes, then heal by vibration.

LEADERSHIP

Carrying or using the Blue Topaz for 6 hours a day, for five days a week, will increase confidence in your leadership skills due to changes in attitude.

LEG CLAMP

Place hematite on the affected area and turn the crystal first clockwise and then counterclockwise, alternating between the two until the cramps disappear.

LET'S GO

Take the transparent quartz and hold it with both hands. Focus on the topics you want to let go of. Turn all your thoughts, energy, and emotions into this quartz and let it take care of everything. Go outside and fill the quartz in an unobstructed place for seven days. Don't forget to mark the area you filled! Let quartz and Mother Earth solve these energies and the problems you gave them. Don't forget to discover the quartz after seven days and clean it thoroughly!

LIGHT SENSITIVITY

Use Rhodonite on your dominant hand or ankle opposite your wrist to resolve light sensitivity issues.

SUMMARY OF LIFE

Use life surrounding Celestite for life overview sessions. You need at least eight crystals to form a circle. If you want to increase your energy production, you can add more.

ABILITY TO LISTEN
Improve your listening skills by carrying Cerussite for seven consecutive days.

LIVER
For liver problems, use a combination of aquamarine and yellow topaz. Lying on your stomach, ask someone to place both stones on your solar plexus chakra and relax for 15 minutes. Be sure to clean up the crystal when you finish your session. Repeat as many times as you need.

LEVER POINT
For best results, make Citrine Yellow Topaz Gem Elixir, charge for 1 hour, and slowly spray all melasma three times a day.

SOLITUDE
Carry or use cobalt iron to combat the issue of loneliness. If you have this problem when

you are at home, also place it in two opposite corners of the main living room. Clean it regularly.

LONG LIFE

If someone wants to extend his life expectancy and live longer, wear or use moonstone whenever possible, especially during the full moon. You can also place moonstones in every room of your home or office. Remember to clean it regularly.

LOST AND DISCOVERED

Charge infinity to find your lost item. Hold it in your hand and focus only on the object you are looking for. Don't get lost in your heart. Follow your intuition when looking for lost purposes.

ROCK RACK/GAMBLING

When playing a lottery game, make sure you have Aventurine, especially in your dominant hand, purse, or near your wallet.

LOVE

Use Rhodonite for seven days, as close to the heart chakra as possible. Remember to clean up the crystal every seven days.

Place the Sardonyx in the corner of your room, closest to your bed, and in the corner closest to your kitchen stove and watch the changes emerge in a few days!

LOVE (UNCONDITIONAL)

Grab Jade and Rose Quartz and focus all your intentions on the subject in question. Carry or use these crystals for the next five days as much as possible. After five days, be sure to clean the crystals and recharge with this procedure. Repeat as many times as you want in different areas of love!

LOYALTY

Loyalty issues have solved with the vibration levels of Kyanite. Please clean this crystal properly before carrying it close to your body or using it. Changes will begin to appear in a few days! If you have a problem with another person's loyalty, post it at home or in the office to see if the change has reflected in that person within a few days.

LUCIDO SLEEP

If you are working in a session with a lucid dream, remember to carry a part-time job in the Orbit field or use it to improve your mental state during the course.

LUCK

All that changes your luck is wearing a single-pointed smoky quartz pendant pointing up. You can also place this crystal in a water spray bottle for 20 minutes to lightly spray your body or area.

LIGHT

Lying down, place indicolite quartz on both sides of the body near the lungs. Then place a clear quartz crystal in the upward heart chakra and take a deep breath for 15 minutes.

LUPUS

To alleviate the symptoms of lupus, use a combination of hematite, clear quartz, and rhodonite in your pocket, handbag, or pendant.

CREATING A NEW PATTERN

Make a purple rainbow fluorspar gem elixir, charge it for 3 hours and gently spray it into your home or office area. Repeat every seven days as the energy pattern changes.

MEN'S ENERGY BALANCE

Make a Green Tourmaline Gem Elixir, charge it for 2 hours and spray it lightly on your entire home or office, especially in the corners.

MANIFESTATION
while focusing on your symptoms for 15 minutes, keep Smoky Quartz and Citrine on your dominant hand. Keep it together for the next few days and see how your wishes come true.

MARRIAGE PROBLEMS
Have your husband cleaned, recharged, and book aquamarine for a more connected marriage. Ask your wife to do the same with Rose Quartz. Exchange both and carry the opposite crystal with you for seven days. Repeat as needed to build a healthy relationship.

MATURE

Carry or use malachite to foster a more mature attitude at work, at home, and in relationships.

MEASLES
To alleviate the symptoms of measles, make a carnelian and hematite gem elixir, charge it for 1 hour and gently spray it from head to toe three times a day.

MEDITATION
For a more enhanced meditation session, surround yourself with another amethyst and clear crystal before starting the course. Make sure everyone points and cleans every seven days.

MEMORIES
To release the painful old memory, place the hematite at your feet, in a relaxed or meditative state, with rose quartz in both

hands. Focus on the mind and release all emerging emotions and feelings.

MENOPAUSE

Carry a combination of Black Onyx and Howlite in your pocket or purse to help relieve menopausal symptoms.

MENTAL ATTACHMENT

Lying down, place yellow ghost quartz on both sides of the head and fluorspar in the third eye chakra. Relax and rest for 15 minutes.

MENTAL CAPACITY

Meditate or sleep with Opal to improve your mental capacity. This enables you to harness the power of your brain with each use.

MENTAL CLEANSER

Mental cleansing is done with lapis lazuli. Lie on your back, one on each side of your head and one in your crown chakra. Breathe slowly, deeply and slowly for 15 minutes. You can also sit in a chair, take your lapis lazuli with your dominant hand, and move clockwise around your head, third eye, and crown chakra to work slowly with crystal energy. Don't forget to clean the crystals later!

MERIDIAN CLEANING AND MARUMA

Use Lodestone in your Meridian and Maluma cleansing sessions to enhance healing and cleansing abilities.

METABOLISM

To enhance your metabolism, fill the bathwater with Amazonite and take a warm bath before starting your day!

MIGRAINE

Lying down, place Tianjin Aura Quartz on each side of the throat. Place one transparent quartz on top of the third eye chakra and another on top of the crown chakra. Relax for 15 minutes and repeat as needed.

MIRROR ENERGY

Mirror energy is when you capture the moods and emotions of others. This can be solved using hematite. I don't know when this will happen, so keep it in your pocket or purse for the best results. Hematite helps to divert, rather than absorb, these energies.

DISCOMFORT

To correct your life's misfortune, take out the black tourmaline and work slowly on all the aura fields to bring out all the negative and stagnant energy.

MONEY

To attract more money to your life, carry pyrite in your wallet or checkbook, and your money will begin to increase.

CHANGES IN HUMOUR

For typical mood swings, use Jet to rebalance and stabilize your mood and emotions. Sit with your feet flat on the ground and hold them with both hands. Focus on all the feelings and emotions that are changing in your life now. Feel like it's changing everywhere. Open your hands quickly and drop the jet on the ground. Take a deep breath, get up, and clean it thoroughly!

MOON ENERGY

Wear moonstones on the ankles before, during, and after the new moon and full moon to enhance the vibrational connection with the moon's energy.

KINETOSIS

Alleviate the symptoms by carrying the aquamarine in your pocket or with your dominant hand during motion sickness.

MOTIVATION

To get more motivated, at work or home, you can put your Carnelian at a place where you spend most of your time.

MOTOR SKILLS

To improve athletic performance, wear or use quartz and mica for seven consecutive days. Remember to clean up the crystal after seven days.

MOUTH

Use a combination of lapis lazuli and rose quartz for mouth problems. Lying down, place the lapis lazuli on the throat chakra and rose quartz crystals on both sides of the mouth and relax for 10 minutes at a time.

MUSCLE CRAMPS

Make Amazonite Gem Elixir, charge for 30 minutes, and lightly spray the affected muscles twice a day. You can also use this water and a few drops in your cream or ointment. The right solution is to place this crystal within 2 inches of the affected area and turn clockwise to extract the negative energy.

MYTHOLOGY

Wear Rainforest Jasper around both ankles to address the prevailing myths about you and your lifestyle.

NAIL GROWTH

Use obsidian to help your nails grow more durable, longer, and faster. Gently rub your nails with this crystal three times a day. Make charged water and put a few drops on each nail three times a day for faster results.

NAUSEA

Lying down, place the topaz on your stomach, and set clear crystals on both sides of your abdomen. Breathe slowly and deeply for 10 minutes.

NARROW NECK

Place the Chrysoprase on your dominant hand and slowly rotate your entire neck. Then turn the crystal clockwise. Then put the crystal back in your dominant hand and twist it over the channel. Finally, rotate the crystal counterclockwise.

NEGATIVITY

To correct the negative vibration, try using black and green tourmaline. It has to be located in one corner of your home, car, or office area. Be sure to clean it twice a month.

FAULT

Wear hematite and rose quartz on the pendant to address the issue of neglect.

NERVOUS

You can wear turquoise as a beautiful piece of jewelry, and no one will know it is there to help with this problem. The necklace is perfect for this situation, as it is relatively focused on the body.

NERVOUS SYSTEM

Use amber and black tourmaline together on the pendant to repair nervous system problems.

NEW BEGINNING

If you want to start over, make a Moonstone Jewel Elixir. Charge for 3 hours and gently spray on all areas to start over. It is best to do on the new moon.

NEW ENVIRONMENT

Put the brown jade in every room and office of your new home to adapt to the new environment and vibration of energy.

NIGHTMARE

Sleep with a combination of amethyst and flour sparing under the pillow to deal with nightmares.

NIGHT SWEAT

You are putting Indicolite Quartz under the pillow to help you absorb night sweats.

NOSE

Lay the fluorspar on the nose, the clear crystal under the nose, and relax for 10 minutes to relieve symptoms.

BLEEDING NOSE

If you have a nosebleed, put sapphire or carnelian over your bridge of the nose to stop the bleeding.

CHAKRA ADJUSTMENT NOTIFICATION

Place a black onyx in each chakra area. Start from the root chakra and pass through the crown chakra. You will feel numbness. Use crystals alternatively between numb areas with hematite and petrified wood. Relax 15 minutes at a time, rest, and take a deep breath. Clean every 15 minutes.

NUTRITION

Use Moonstone to experience a more luxurious side. Place it in a high-usage location or in multiple locations in your home for wearing and carrying.

OBJECTIVITY

Place Rainforest Jasper in the two facing corners of your home or office where you spend the most time solving this problem.

OBSESSION
Wear or use white spirit quartz to control obsessive-compulsive problems.

OPEN THE HEART
Lay the Aragonite stones and place it on the third chakra for 20 minutes a day, and each time you do this, you will open up to more fantastic possibilities.

FRANK
To be more open to ideas, people and situations, carry or use Astrophyllite for seven consecutive days. Don't forget to clean up the crystal later.

OPTIMISM
Want to be more optimistic? For the most effective results, wear a chalcedony around your neck!

ORGANIZATIONAL SKILLS

Organizing is not for everyone, but you can use Jasper to improve your organizing skills. Place it in two opposite corners of your office or home. Here you will do most of the organization, and your skills will improve dramatically.

IN-BODY EXPERIENCE (OBE)

If you're interacting with an in-vitro experience during a session, use Apophyllite to improve your experience and connectivity.

REACTION PROBLEMS

If you are one of those who tend to overreact to everyday situations, try carrying Moonstone as part of your daily life. Moonstone helps calm your emotional reaction!

OVERSTIMULATION

Lying down, place the blue quartz on the heart chakra and breathe deeply for 15 minutes to soothe the overstimulation.

THINK TOO MUCH

Create a howlite grid in a small area close to where you usually think about the problem, such as your office or home table. Make sure you are near the locality where you are most experiencing the reversal of the effect.

PAIN

Use a combination of turquoise and rose quartz to reduce joint pain from injuries and illnesses. Place them near the affected area for 5 minutes and aim directly at the location of the pain. Then slowly rotate the crystal clockwise for another 2 minutes. This helps pull out local negative energy and resume positive energy flow to relieve pain. Continue to use the two alternately until the pain subsides.

PALPITATION

Hold your hematite and rose quartz over your heart chakra with your dominant hand and breathe slowly for 15 minutes to resolve the pounding problem.

PANCREAS

Lying on your stomach, place two emeralds, one on each side of the center, and place smoky quartz in the center. Take a break and relax for 15 minutes. Repeat as needed.

PANIC ATTACK

Pick up the green Ghost Quartz with both hands and sit down. Close your eyes, relax your hands on your knees, and breathe deeply and slowly for 15 minutes to relieve the panic attack.

PARANOIA

Use a combination of hematite and sugilite to address the delusion problem.

PARTICIPATION

If you're having trouble with engagement issues, place four clusters of clear crystals, one in the corner of the room where you spend most of your time. Be sure to clean it twice a month.

PASSION

Be sure to use Garnet for anyone and any situation that requires passion!

PASSIVE ENERGY PROBLEMS

For passive energy issues, wear Blue Jade around your right ankle for five consecutive days.

PAST HEALING

Use Tanzanite during past healing sessions to improve the work done.

THE MEMORY OF PAST LIFE

Use Amber to relive your memories and past life problems. Wear the crystal and increase the effectiveness in past life and meditation sessions.

PATIENCE

Patience issues can be solved by Lord Knight. It helps bring vibration levels to your most relaxing behavior. Make an elixir with it, charge the water base for 1 hour, and gently spray from head to toe, where needed.

PEACE

For best results, make rose quartz gems and blue tourmaline elixirs. Charge the water base for 1 hour and lightly spray it wherever peace is desired. If you need a calm home and living environment, spread it everywhere in your home.

STILLNESS OF SPIRIT

Wear the sapphire pendant and rest assured when you have a hard time.

PERCEPTION
Put Desert Rose in your pocket to raise awareness of ideas, places, people, and situations.

INDIVIDUAL POWER
Wear a combination of garnet and emerald around your heart chakra for two days to enhance your strength.

PESSIMISTIC BEHAVIOUR
Wear or carry the hawk's eyes to combat suspicious behavior. If emotion occurs in a work-like area, place two, one on each diagonal of the room.

PHOBIA
Carry the blue opal in your pocket or purse to treat the phobia you experience. When you experience phobia, pull it out and gently

bring it closer to the heart chakra and take a deep breath.

PLANT ENERGY
Wear moss agate around the ankle to connect with the energy of the plant!

PLANT GROWTH
Place cerates in potted plants or wrap them with this crystal to prevent pests and stimulate root growth. Make elixir, charge for 1 hour, and water plants with this elixir as needed.

POISON IVY RASH
When you touch the poison ivy, and the itchy rash starts to appear, make black tourmaline and aventurine gem elixir and charge for 30 minutes. Spray gently from head to toe as much as you need!

POSSIBILITY

Wear Poppy Jasper for a day's well-being, positivity, and overall feeling!

POSTPARTUM PROBLEM
To deal with Baby Blue, use Rhodonite for the pendant and Black Onyx as an anklet for best results.

ANIMAL POWER COMMUNICATION
For power animal communication sessions, wear a combination of Sherman Phantom Quartz and Dalmatian stones to improve the connection.

PRACTICAL SENSE
Is there a practical problem? Wearing one tiger's eye on your left ankle or wrist for three days, these problems begin to change!

PREMATURE AGING

Make a turquoise gem elixir, charge it for 1 hour and gently splash it in the area you want to fight the signs of aging.

CURRENT ENERGY

Need help to be here? Let's carry Staurolite, also called Fairy Cross, in your pocket!

PROBLEM

Create a Red Jasper Gem Elixir, charge it for 1 hour and gently spray it on all areas of your home or office to repel problems before they even occur. This is to present a potential issue that may not have been known so far and has to be addressed before it gets out of hand.

ENERGY PROJECTION

Use yellow jasper to project energy during a healing session. Before you start, make sure it's in your dominant hand and is connected firmly. This is useful when working in individual healing sessions and making more reliable energy connections.

PROPHECY

Using emeralds, in combination with strengthening exercises, will enhance your prophetic skills! Use it to meditate, channel or use as close to your third eye chakra as possible to surround yourself. While lying down, place an emerald on the third chakra and start meditation.

PROSPERITY

Hold the Ammonite in your pocket, purse, or purse and enhance the atmosphere of wellbeing.

PROTECTION

Black tourmaline and onyx are excellent for protection. They help the ground and repel negative energy. The best suggestion is, use one to wear as a pendant and one as an anklet. It lands, repels, and protects from all negative energy and problems.

MENTAL ATTACK

To prevent and avoid psychic attacks, carry or use Aqua Aura.

MENTAL DEVELOPMENT

Lapis lazuli, amethyst, and quartz are an instrumental combination for improving mental development. Lay on your back and place a lapis lazuli on the throat chakra, an amethyst on the third eye chakra, and a clear crystal on the crown chakra. Stay focused and meditate on your intentions during this time. You can also carry and use these crystal combinations to bring that ability to the aura field at all times. Surrounding yourself with alternating crystals in a circle during a traditional meditation session is also a big plus!

PUBLIC STATEMENT

Don't forget to bring Hematite and Carnelian together during the conversation to solve the problem.

PURE THOUGHT

Lie down and place Azurite on your third eye chakra for 15 minutes to gain pure, in-depth access to your subconscious mind and thoughts.

PURIFICATION

Create an Elixir of Smoky Quartz Gem and charge it for 2 hours to lightly moisten your body from head to toe or moisturize the whole body.

NO SMOKING

Carry or use Botswana agate as an additional boost to help stop smoking.

ANGER

Carry or use a Carnelian to combat the emotions of anger. Wear this on your dominant side for the best results.

RAINBOW ENERGY

To improve your rainbow energy connection, try using Rainbow Fluorite during your session.

QUICK CHANGE

For a rapid change, make a clear moldavite and quartz elixir and gently spray it on all areas of your home or office. Then place moldavite and clear quartz on the opposite end of the house to increase the vibrational energy.

RASH

For best results, make a red strip of agate gem elixir charged for 1 hour and splash it lightly on the eruption area 3 times a day.

RATIONALITY

Sodalite has used for thoughtful questions. Wear or use this crystal during this time!

RAZOR LIGHT BULB
Gently rub Rhodonite Gem Elixir for 30 minutes on the razor ridge three times a day.

PERFORMANCE ISSUES
Using amethyst as close as possible to the heart chakra will cause performance issues.

RECEIVE ENERGY
To receive energy from a person or session, put transparent quartz in your dominant hand or your dominant hand to enhance reception.

RECOVERY FROM ILLNESS
Make sure there is as much water as possible around the person recovering from the disease. This speeds up the healing process. Please clean it daily.

RECOVERY FROM SURGERY

When recovering from surgery, be sure to wear turquoise, oak marine, and clear crystal from a person or room that you spend most of your time with. Please clean it daily.

REGENERATION

For playback issues, use the Heavenly Quartz gem elixir, which charges for 2 hours. For best results, lightly spray your entire body.

HOW TO IMPROVE REIKI

To increase Reiki's energy, be sure to include Pink Crackle Quartz in every session. Surround yourself or hold it in your hand when working.

REINTEGRATION

Eilat stone is used for energy integration. Please be sure to bring it with you for five consecutive days.

REJECT

For best results, charge for 1 hour to make a carnelian and rose quartz gem elixir. In addition to these problems, gently spray your entire body from head to toe once a day for areas that cause rejection problems.

REJUVENATION

Make Purpurite Gem Elixir, charge it for 1 hour and gently spray it where needed.

THROW THE PAST

Hold Azurite and focus only on the past problems you want to release. Focus all your energy on these thoughts and intentions, and the vibrational energy of azurite will capture and free them. Be sure to clean it after use.

RELEASE

Wear a phantom quartz crystal and wear it on your neck for five days to solve the problem.

RELATIONSHIP

Try a combination of malachite and rose quartz. They bring happiness, love, respect, and calming relaxing energy. Wear them at these times or have them together and watch the relationship grow!

ABOLISH LOW ENERGY

Put hematite and smoky quartz in your pocket when you're out and repel low vibration energy.

SETTLEMENT PROBLEM

Malachite, attached to the long-chain pendant at the time of resentment, alleviates these problems!

CONCERNS

Take a warm Bloodstone bath to soothe your restlessness.

REFEREE DEPARTMENT SYNDROME

Fight the restless leg syndrome by using the hawk's eyes around the ankle at bedtime.

RESURRECTION

Create an Elixir of Carnelian, Citrine, Clear Crystal Gem, charge it for 2 hours, and gently spray it on the area, person, or item in need of help.

RHEUMATISM

Combine amber and carnelian to relieve rheumatism. Charge these two in a water base for 30 minutes and gently spray onto the affected area.

ROOM CLEANING

Make an amber gem elixir, charge it for 1 hour and gently spray it on all areas from the ceiling to the floor of the room, including everything in the place except furniture, corners, and appliances.

ROSACEA
Make an amethyst and citrine gem elixir, charge for 1 hour, and slowly spray all affected areas three times a day.

SADNESS
Wear Indigo Light Quartz and Rose Quartz on the pendant near the heart chakra for seven days. Don't forget to clean thoroughly.

SCABS
Make a gem elixir with carnelian and cobaltite, charge for 2 hours, and lightly touch or moisten the affected area.

SHORT

Surround yourself with a combination of emeralds and hematite to combat the feelings and problems of scarcity.

SCAR
Make Kovalite Gem Elixir, charge it for 1 hour, then tap the charged water gently on the scar. Repeat as many times as you need.

SCATTERED ENERGY
Wear hematite around your ankles to deal with the distributed energy. For even more boost, wear it on your other wrist!

REACHING OUT
Improve your skills and observation sessions with Celestite groups.

SEASONAL AFFECTIVE DISORDER

Use Septarian during times when affected by SAD. Remember to clean this every three day.

SAFETY

Make the agate jewel elixir of wood agar, charge it for 1 hour and spray it safely to the problematic area or person. Repeat as many times as you need.

SELF-CARE

Carry or use Epidote as often as you can and receive gentle reminders to keep you fit by resting, eating healthy, and exercising.

AUTOMATIC CONTROL

Wear Gray Hawkeye in case of loss of control.

SELF-ESTEEM ISSUE

To solve the problem of self-esteem, carry or use chalcopyrite for seven consecutive days.

SELF-DESTRUCTIVE PROBLEMS

The combination of smoky quartz and citrine is effective when tackling self-destructive problems. Carry these two together or use them for maximum benefit!

SELF-CURE

Amber is a great way to promote someone's self-healing! Place it on the affected area for 20 minutes. If you're working on general self-healing, this should fix it before you start your session.

OWN LOVE

Tackle the problem of self-love with a rose quartz pendant as close as possible to your heart chakra. You can also recharge the bathtub with water for 20 minutes and increase this self-loved vibration energy with a warm and relaxing bath.

RESPECT YOURSELF

Improve your self-esteem with a combination of Rainforest Jasper and Rose Quartz for seven days.

SELF-ESTIMATION PROBLEM
Bring Howlite close to the heart chakra once a day for seven days, focusing on selfish, oppositional, and non-critical issues.

FEEL COMMUNICATION
When trying to communicate with whales, dolphins, etc., wear moldavite. If this doesn't allow you to meditate around yourself, use it as close as possible to your throat chakra for the best results.

SERENITY
Make an amethyst gem elixir, charge it for 30 minutes, and then lightly spray it. Remove the amethyst and place it in the corner of the same room.

SEXUAL IMPROVEMENT
Place red jasper in all four corners of the room and smoky quartz under the bed to enhance sexuality.

SHAMAN JOURNEY
Mochi balls placed in a circle around you during your shamanic journey will improve your connection and your journey!

SHELTER ENERGY
Place lapis lazuli and clear quartz in one corner of each room where protective energy is needed. Remember to clean it twice a month.

SHOCK PROBLEM
For everyone, a concussion can be a catastrophic blow to the aura field. Lying down, place the hematite on the foot chakra, the carnelian on the navel, the turquoise on

the throat chakra, and the transparent quartz on the crown chakra and the two-handed chakra. Take a break and relax for 30 minutes.

TENSION SHOULDER

You can relieve tension and pressure on your shoulders by keeping the chrysoprase 2 inches away from the affected area. Turn this clockwise to remove the negative energy trace.

SHYNESS

Especially if you are shy and want to get out of the shell, carry or use a Lepidore light. It can take several days to pass some thicker energy, so be patient!

SIMPLICITY

Create a Larimar Jewel Elixir, charge it for 30 minutes, and lightly spray it not only on yourself but in the areas, you want to simplify.

SING

Wear Rhodonite on the pendant around your neck to enhance your singing skills!

THE PROBLEM OF SINUSITIS

Make Eilat Stone Gem Elixir and charge it for 1 hour. You can then gently pat the area in need of healing with a vibrating crystal or steam this electrically charged water to inhale to heal it from the inside.

SKIN IRRITATION / PROBLEM

Make a clear turquoise quartz crystal gem elixir, charge it for 1 hour and gently spray it on the area of skin where you need help.

SLEEP PROBLEMS (CHILDREN)

For nightmare, boogie man, and monster problems in closets or under the bed, place Charoite under the ground or in the closet where these horrors plague the child. You can also get rid of the devils that scare your kids by having your kids make monster repellent sprays. Put water in showers for 30 minutes and let your little kid spray all the bad guys!

TALK ABOUT DREAMS
Place rainbow fluorite under a person's pillow before going to sleep to reduce conversation problems.

SLEEPWALKING
Have a rainbow moonstone worn before bedtime to resolve sleep problems.

SNORE
For snoring problems, place lapis lazuli in the two opposite corners of the bed frame and clear quartz in the two different edges of the bed frame to solve the snoring problem.

SOVIET

Try to use as much iolite as possible around your throat chakras to keep you drinking and increase your strength and courage.

SOCIALIZATION

To improve your social skills, keep Garnet every time you have a chance to socialize!

SORE THROAT

Make a blue crystal elixir, charge for 1 hour, then rinse with charged water. Repeat as many times as you need.

PAINFUL

Use Carnelian to relieve body pain. Place it within 2 inches of the problem, rotate clockwise first, then counterclockwise, then turn the two alternately. Don't forget to clean thoroughly afterward.

HEAL THE SOUL

Wear black opal during your soul healing session to establish a secure connection and allow your clients or yourself to maximize the potential of your actual soul value.

PURPOSE OF THE SOUL

Bring the Chiastolitic, also known as the Cross Stone, when looking for the soul. This helps to promote vibrational energy in this area. During a meditation session, four people can surround themselves to find an answer.

SOUL RECOVERY

For the most striking effect, use crystal lepidocrocite during the Soul Recovery session.

ENERGY FLOW RATE

Putting a tiger's eye around both ankles will allow faster energy flow through the chakras, aura, and meridians.

SPIRITUAL AWAKENING
Surround yourself with fluorspar during a meditation session and sleep with the same crystals under the pillow to connect with them. Carry one of them for seven days and watch the spiritual awakening session begin.

SPIRITUAL BLOCK
Wear Star Ruby when working on the spiritual path to clearing obstacles. These blocks can come in any shape along your way, so keep your Star Ruby in your necklace, pocket, or as close to you as possible at your home or office.

SPIRITUAL CLEANSER

Use Lapis Lazuli for seven consecutive days to improve the spiritual cleanliness of your soul.

SPONTANEITY
Have the person wear Opole on the dominant side for at least two days to increase voluntary behavior.

SPRAIN
Make Dalmatian Stone Gem Elixir, charge for 1 hour, and soak the twisted area. If you cannot absorb the affected area, then soak a clean towel in charged water and wrap it around the area. Then take the Dalmatian stone, place it within 2 inches of the sprain, and turn clockwise to remove any remaining negative energy.

STABILITY
Wear a combination of Fadden Quartz and Amber to increase the stability of your life.

SCENIC HORROR
Be sure to put the Dumortierite in your pocket before you enter the stage. By doing so, you can reach out and hold it in your hands frequently, increasing your vibration energy even further.

STUTTERING
To tackle stuttering problems, wear blue tourmaline near your throat chakra, if possible.

STATIONARY
Make Celestite Gem Elixir and lightly spray all areas where quietness is required.

GASTRIC ULCER
For the problem of gastric ulcers; place agate on the belly, with two clear crystals facing inward, one on each side of the body. Relax for 15 minutes and repeat as needed.

STORM

For power protection during a storm, place an agate in every room of your home, or use it if you're traveling out during a storm.

STRENGTH

If you are weak or need more power, wear agate with a red band around your ankles for the best results.

STRESS

Use amethyst to reduce stress levels. You can place it around your home or office, fill it with fog, use it, or put it on your body.

TESTARUDEZ

Combine rose quartz and malachite to alleviate stubborn problems.

STUDY

To improve your learning skills, be sure to carry your sodalite with you during the study session.

ORZUELO

Hold 2 inches of fluorspar from the affected eye area. Rotate it three times clockwise. Next, hold the clear crystal 2 inches from your eye and rotate it three times clockwise. Other two crystals for 5 minutes 3 times a day.

SUBCONSCIOUS

Use Selenite for mental issues. Starting with holding it, you visualize it by lowering the energy of the white light passing through the crown chakra, reaching the body, and passing through the root chakra. Then place it on top of the third chakra to hold the information stored in the subconscious.

SOLAR ENERGY

Wear sunstone around the ankle, 24 hours a day, for three days to improve the vibrational connection to solar energy.

TANNED

Make Dumortierite Gem Elixir, charge it for 1 hour and gently spray it on all sunburned areas.

SUPPORT ISSUES

Dark Citrine is useful in support issues. If you're missing someone's support, put it in your home or office where you spend most of your time. If you are not providing sufficient support to others, wear this, or carry it with you.

SUPPRESSED PATTERN

Use Apache tears during a meditation or healing session, placing one in each hand and one in each foot chakra to reveal the suppressed pattern.

TRANSPIRATION

For excessive sweating, make an elixir of emerald, carnelian, or bright crystal gem and charge for one hour. First, gently spray your body from head to toe. Then lightly spray a layer of an aura surrounding your institution within 2 feet to alleviate these problems.

SWELLING

Place the aquamarine 2 inches from the bulge area and turn it counterclockwise and then clockwise to reduce swelling.

YEAR SWIMMER

Lying down, place the hematite on the throat chakra, the transparent crystal on the crown chakra, and the fluorspar on both sides of the ear. Relax for 20 minutes to relieve pressure and pain.

TALENT

Boost your talent with Bloodstone. Wear or use this as much as possible when focusing on the issue of your ability.

TEACH
Bring or use citrine to enhance your capacity and energy in the education sector.

TOOTH
For a healthy tooth, fill a glass of water with Fluorite for 15 minutes and rinse your mouth and teeth with this charged water.

TELEPATHY
Hold Angelite against the third chakra when using telepathic skills to improve connectivity and transmission.

TENDINITIS
Lie down and surround yourself with alternating crystals of transparent quartz, rose quartz, and black tourmaline. For Gem Elixirs, soak these three stones for 1 hour and spray all affected areas.

VOLTAGE

Place the black tourmaline 2 inches from the tensed area and move it up and down several times. When the stress is relieved, turn it clockwise to squeeze out the remaining stagnation and force.

THOUGHT
Use Celestite to improve your thoughts. Carry as much as you can, or post to the office or home where you spend most of your time.

THROAT INFECTION
To alleviate throat infections, add a crystal of aquamarine and gargle three times a day.

TMJ
Lying down, place three hematite stones around the jawline. One on the base and one on each side. Then place one amethyst on

each side of the ear and one on top of the third eye chakra. Relax 20 minutes at a time.

TOLERANCE
Take or use a Chrysoprase and place it on two diagonals in your home or office to mitigate resistance issues.

GRINDING PAIN
For toothaches, soak aquamarine in a bowl of water for 20 minutes. Gently rub charged water on tooth and gum lines or rinse the mouth with charged water.

TRANSLATE THOUGHTS
Hold this in your dominant hand and use Cerussite during a meditation session. Remember to record everything after the meeting. This will help you translate higher thinking into this physical plane, so have a Cirrus in your hand.

TRAUMA

The combination of aqua aura and rose quartz gives the best results in trauma situations. Carry this near your body or surround yourself with them and get rid of the negative energy.

TRAVEL PROTECTION

For essential travel protection, wear or use your Blue Obsidian while traveling.

TREE ENERGY

Use the Tree Agate to land and connect to tree energy. Hold this in your hand and select the tree you like. If possible, walk barefoot and hug the tree. Sit at the root of the tree and enjoy the power connection.

TREE GROWTH

Place the tree and moss agate around the root of the tree and insert the two alternately to promote the growth of the tree. Make the gem elixir, charge it for 1 hour, and water the tree with this elixir as needed.

TRUST ISSUES

Reliability problems have solved by wearing hematite. This reflects negative matters so you can focus on distracting energy during these hours.

TRUTH

Carrying or using Iolite as much as possible causes real problems in certain situations. If you are looking for the truth of another person, place iolite in the four corners of the room where both of you spend hours.

TWIN FLAME

Have blue aragonite near the heart chakra and program it to attract the twin flames. Please carry this with you as much as possible.

UNCOMFORTABLE FEELING

If uncomfortable, look for clear quartz, rose quartz, and amethyst. Keep them near your heart chakra and release all the unpleasant feelings and take a deep breath. If you have them all, surround yourself with them to immediately release this energy.

UNDERSTANDING

Wear lapis lazuli on a pendant very close to the heart chakra to help understand the problem.

UNDERWORLD

Use the Smoky Spirit Quartz in meditation and channeling sessions to circle yourself and strengthen your connection to the underground world.

URINARY TRACT

Lying down, place Tianjin Aura Quartz on the lower abdomen, Carnelian, on both sides of the body and Hematite on foot for 15 minutes.

UNIQUE PERSONAL ENERGY

When working in a group, create a Labradorite Gem Elixir, charge it one hour in advance, and gently spray it into the area. This helps each one to make their energy to share with the world.

A UNIQUE WAY OF LIFE

Find or create your life path by carrying or using Amazonite as much as possible.

INVISIBLE ENTITIES

Place Prehnite around your house, in every corner, for invisible entities. You can take it and use it to solve these problems even if you are not at home.

UNNECESSARY ENERGY

For unwanted energy, use Sugilite with two opposite ends in the same room as your home or office.

EXCELLENT CHAKRA
When you open the upper chakra, make sure you have purple agate around it. If you want to do this with your guide and higher self, meditate on Purple Agate.

VARICOSE VEIN
Make a yellow topaz gem elixir, charge for one hour, slowly spray varicose veins twice a day for seven days, and watch it begin to heal.

VIBRATION ENERGY
Make sure you are wearing petalite, especially if you want to feel more of the strength of vibrations with crystals and gems. Hold this in your dominant hand while healing

or handling crystal or other vibrational energy.

VIRUS
When fighting an infection, bring the apatite as close as possible to the heart chakra to speed up the healing process.

VISION
Transparent calcite helps magnify vision problems. Sleep with it under the pillow, meditate while it is around your body, or lie down and keep it between your eyes, just below the third eye chakra.

VISION QUESTIONS
For best results, surround yourself with a petalite circle during your vision search session.

VISUALIZATION

Focusing on the visualization adds selenite to increase the potential. Surround yourself with them for higher levels of vibration.

ENHANCED VOICE
Put your used Carnelian around your neck and put your chakra in your throat to make your voice stronger.

WARTS / MOLES
Make a marcasite elixir and charge for 2 hours. If necessary, gently spray or tap the area with charged water.

WATER LOAD
Hold the finished clear crystal in your hand and slowly rotate it three times clockwise over the drinking water to wash away the toxins.

WATER ENERGY

Brings or uses a combination of aqua aura and aquamarine to enhance the energy vibration of water for seven days.

WATER/SAFETY JOURNEY
Carry or use Aquamarine on your body for travel and water safety.

WATERY EYE
Lying down, place the iolite on each eye and aim the clear quartz crystal on the third eye for 10 minutes. Repeat as needed.

WEIGHT GAIN
To gain weight, use amber and add it 10 minutes before meals to increase the level of vibration.

WEIGHT LOSS
Lose weight with the combination of Moonstone and Rose Quartz. Charge your food 10 minutes before meals and bring

these crystals with you. Combine welfare turquoise and ammonite to boost the energy of wellness around you for seven days.

COMPLETENESS
When you lie down, place the Eilat Stone in the solar plexus chakra, condition your mind and body, and feel again as a whole.

DO
Tiger Eye is an excellent booster of willpower. For best results, wear this around your wrist with your dominant hand.

WORKING ENVIRONMENT
Place a group of amethyst in your work environment to keep energy flowing, clean, and positive for everyone entering this space.

INCREDIBLE PROBLEM
When you're worried, hold Lepidolite in your hand and focus on your positive results.

SCRATCH

Use Carnelian and Celestite to dress the wound less than 2 inches from the injury and remove the damage by moving the two clockwise, then counterclockwise. Don't forget to clean thoroughly afterward. If possible, place them on both sides of the injury and direct the energy from one side to the other.

COMPULSIVE WORKER

Create Tree Agate Gemstone, Rose Quartz, and Amber Elixirs, charge them for 2 hours, and once weekly, gently spray them across the work addict's working area to reduce the work time.

WRITING

To improve your writing ability, try sodalite, whether you're tying on your dominant wrist or anywhere else. If you have an office, place it on the deck or work area.

BALANCE

Carry or wear Eilat Stone for seven days to balance the energy of Yin and Yang as much as possible.

Here is an overview of what to do with crystals and what not to do. The more detail you learn about healing crystals, the better it works for your body. Understanding what to do and what not to do is essential to getting the best crystals. Instead of worrying about how to get the best crystals for effective crystal healing, use the following as a guide. What to do If your friends recommend jewelry or crystals, make sure you know why they keep supporting them. Stay in apperception that the higher knowledge you get, the faster and better the healing process. For example, if my mother told me to wear pearls to relieve my anger and anxiety, I would probably do so at my mother's request. But if you know how it relates to the birth chart and moon placement, you can quickly get better results. With your knowledge, you can become more reliable and gain moon energy. Do not use any crystals immediately after purchase. Clean them up first and follow the exact performance method.

Washing methods vary from overnight soaking in saltwater, un-boiled milk, or running water. Before using crystals, always ask the seller how to remove traces and energy from them. Do not get angry if crystals or stones fall, break, or get lost. Most crystal healers believe that once that happens, the work has done. This gives energy to the crystal. You can do this by asking an astrologer or healer for help. This helps a lot to make crystals and gemstones work for you. Do not wear earrings, necklaces, and rings at the same time if you witness a crystal bracelet or pendant has given good results. If you do this, you may overdose. Remember, excesses are dangerous. Always trust your feelings about the crystal. If you think your favorite stones are working ideally and effectively, get them. However, if it is dense, heavy, and uncomfortable, remove the crystals.

Before you completely ignore the crystal, share your concerns with a professional crystal healer first. Follow these recommendations and prohibitions to get the most out of your crystal. You can also find out if you need to find another crystal to get the perfect result. Choosing a Crystal for Healing and finding the ideal crystal for healing is not easy. Before reaching the ideal one, you need to make sure you know its exact function. It's great to use the "first impression" when looking for crystals. As recommended, stand in front of multiple crystals when shopping. Then close your eyes and relax. When you open your eyes, take the crystal, you see first. If you are looking for a crystal for a specific reason, meditation can help you solve your problem. Keep in mind that when looking for a crystal, you must first consider its intent. Remember to seek advice from a crystal healer to ensure you get the ideal type for your purpose. Before you buy, you also need to know which one meets your budget and needs.

Not everyone who uses crystal gets good results. If people don't want to experience the same thing, follow these caveats to make sure the crystal works as expected.

- **Carefully select stones:** Choosing your favorite crystal means trusting your instincts. Crystals are not manufactured at the factory. They are all-natural. Therefore, I don't like finding the perfect size and shape.

- **Clean the crystal:** Cleaning the crystal will restore it to its original state. Do this correctly, especially when your friends are controlling your crystal. Cleaning is done with fire, air, soil, and water.

- **Charge Crystal:** This will help regenerate the crystal and give it energy. You can charge the crystal whenever you want. The more energy you give to the crystal, the more effective it will be. The crystals need to be able to receive sunlight and solar power.
- **Dedicate Crystal:** Dedicating the crystal ensures security for your purposes.
- **Attach yourself to crystal:** To attach, you need to befriend with crystal. By deepening the connection with the crystal, you can get a more positive atmosphere.
- **Keep the crystal in a safe place:** Protect the crystal by placing it in a bag so that you can reach it. Do not leave it packed around your wallet.
- **Wear crystals:** Depending on your intentions, you can use crystals for mental, emotional, and physical problems. It can also be applied to general health and wellness.

CONCLUSION

With the information about crystals, it's easy to select the crystal that best suits your needs. Know which one works best for you and see how it works. No matter what kind of glass you use, just wait for the results to come out. These crystals serve as good luck and guides. If you practice them rightly, sooner or later, you will also witness their amazing results. However, this does not mean that you will always rely on these gems. If you have a hard disability, it is best to seek help from a health care professional. By doing so, you can guarantee your safety. Alternatively, these crystals have also used to treat pets and plants. Crystal Healing Ideas on which you can place your trust are calm, relax, revitalize, heal, dispel negativity, relieve stress, and influence growth. It is also useful in solving problems, balancing, uplifting, and lighting. If you have these crystals, you may not know where to put them. Depending on your choice, you can set the stone in the entrance hall, living room, or dining room.

COPYRIGHTS

© **Copyright 2020 By Cassian Byrd**
All rights reserved

This book
"CRYSTALS FOR BEGINNERS: Meditation Techniques, Reiki and Healing Stones! The Power of Crystal Healing! How to Enhance Your Chakras-Spiritual Balance and Human Energy Field"
Written by Cassian Byrd

This document aims to provide precise and reliable details on this subject and the problem under discussion.

The product is marketed on the assumption that no officially approved bookkeeping or publishing house provides other available funds.

Where a legal or qualified guide is required, a person must have the right to participate in the field.

A statement of principle, which is a subcommittee of the American Bar Association, a committee of publishers and Associations and approved. A copy, reproduction, or distribution of parts of this text, in electronic or written form, is not permitted.

The recording of this Document is strictly prohibited, and any retention of this text is only with the written permission of the publisher and all Liberties authorized.

The information provided here is correct and reliable, as any lack of attention or other means resulting from the misuse or use of the procedures, procedures, or instructions contained therein is the total, and absolute obligation of the user addressed.

The author is not obliged, directly or indirectly, to assume civil or civil liability for any restoration, damage, or loss resulting from the data collected here. The respective authors retain all copyrights not kept by the publisher.

The information contained herein is solely and universally available for information purposes. The data is presented without a warranty or promise of any kind.

The trademarks used are without approval, and the patent is issued without the trademark owner's permission or protection.

The logos and labels in this book are the property of the owners themselves and are not associated with this text.

CPSIA information can be obtained
at www.ICGtesting.com
Printed in the USA
BVHW091917240621
610370BV00002B/170